TRACKING THE

ELUSIVE HUMAN

VOLUME I

TRACKING
THE
ELUSIVE
HUMAN

VOLUME   I
A PRACTICAL GUIDE TO
C.G. JUNG'S PSYCHOLOGICAL TYPES
W.H. SHELDON'S BODY AND
TEMPERAMENT TYPES
AND THEIR INTEGRATION

TYRA ARRAJ and JAMES ARRAJ

INNER GROWTH BOOKS

Copyright © 1988 by Tyra Arraj and James Arraj

Printed in the United States of America.

For ordering information on this and other titles see the back pages or write:
Inner Growth Books
Bos 520
Chiloquin, OR 97624

The authors invite your comments through the above address.

This book is printed on acid free paper.

LIBRARY OF CONGRESS
Library of Congress Cataloging-in-Publication Data

Arraj, Tyra.
    Tracking the elusive human / by Tyra Arraj and James Arraj.
        p.   cm.
    Bibliography: v. 1, p.
    Includes index.
    Contents: v. 1. A practical guide to C.G. Jung's psychological
types, W.H. Sheldon's body and temperament types, and their
integration
    ISBN 0-914073-16-8 (v. 1 : alk. paper)
    1. Typology (Psychology) 2. Difference (Psychology) 3. Jung, C.
G. (Carl Gustav), 1875-1961. 4. Sheldon, William Herbert, 1899-
5. Individuation.   I. Arraj, Jim. II. Title.
BF698.3.A77 1987
155.2'64--dc19   87-30213
                                                        CIP

TO C.G. JUNG

CONTENTS

ACKNOWLEDGEMENTS

Full acknowledgements will be made in **Volume II.** Both volumes contain material that first appeared in **A Tool for Understanding Human Differences,** but in such a different context that both volumes are new works.

We owe to the kindness of Michael Ramus the cartoons and illustrations of physiques that appear in Chapters 4 and 5. He drew them for an article about Sheldon that appeared in the June 25, 1951 issue of Life magazine.

PART I

TRACKING

CHAPTER 1

C.G. JUNG'S
PSYCHOLOGICAL TYPES

The sun filtered through the pines that surround our forest home as I walked along the dusty path and saw written on it the secret story of the night. Here a rabbit had hopped by on his rounds, over there a tiny field mouse had scurried by, and the sharp hooves of a deer had marched up the trail to the salt lick. But there is much of this story I cannot read. One morning a new track appears. What animal made it? Where did it come from? What kind of life does it lead?

Sometimes I wish I had a real tracker with me, someone like Tom Brown who was trained as a child by an Apache, Stalking Wolf. He spent countless hours following tracks, watching them being transformed by wind and weather, and learning the ways of the animals who made them. If Tom Brown were here, I think, I wouldn't be confined to the most obvious signs on my little path. I could learn to see and follow these tracks to their ultimate conclusion.

This winding path makes me think of my own years spent learning to track the most elusive of creatures, the one that hides by standing right in front of us, and conceals himself by leaving a million tracks, the one we assume we already know completely: ourselves. And I learned to track quite by accident, or maybe it was that kind of happy chance that often brings us some of the best things in life.

I had a job, an apartment, a car, a little money in the bank and a circle of friends. I should have been content, but something was missing. People had come into my life - and gone - and I had a faint suspicion that I could have learned something both from the success and failures of those relationships. But just what that lesson was escaped me. My years in school had done little to give me an answer. No one taught me how to get along with people. I took an occasional psychology course, or saw a movie or read a book where the main character faced some sort of psychological dilemma, and a psychiatrist helped him out of it, but nothing I saw or heard spoke to me personally. I wasn't suffering from any mental disorder. I ate well, slept well and seemed to be a success as far as the world was concerned. But it wasn't enough. I needed to find a deeper way of understanding myself and others.

Then I met Jim. Right from the beginning our relationship was different. He had had much the same experiences and had felt the same undefined longing, but one day not long before we met he had come across a book that was to change both our lives. It was C.G. Jung's **Psychological Types.** At first glance this large volume looks exactly like the kind of book that has made psychology irrelevant to so many people. But it isn't. It's really about Jung's own search to make sense out of his own life. Jim somehow felt in a way that he couldn't really articulate or fully understand that this book could help us make sense out of our own lives, too. It encouraged him to read other books by Jung, and the result was that when we went to the park he tried to explain how men and women project on each other and what Jung meant by the anima and animus. Eating bread and cheese on a river bank was accompanied by a discussion of the unconscious. Dinner was topped off by a description of introversion, extraversion and the four functions. Some dates! I had never heard of Jung, but I recognized the words extraversion and introversion. Extraverts were the life of the party, while the introverts were busy being wall flowers. Extraverts were dressed in carefully chosen color-coordinated outfits, while the introverts were discreetly attired in mouse grey or dull brown. Extraverts carried their hearts on their sleeves, while introverts tended to be morbid. To be extraverted was to be a success, but an introvert wasted endless hours alone in melancholic introspection. Extraverts were making touchdowns while introverts were quietly curled up in a corner reading a book. Extraverts quickly caught on to the game of life, while the introverts didn't even seem to know the rules.

Jim was quick to correct my impressions. For Jung both introversion and extraversion were equally acceptable ways of dealing with life, and didn't have much in common with the popular definitions. It was interesting, but I have to admit it all sounded pretty theoretical.

Then one night I had a dream that changed everything. I told it to Jim the next day. I was in my own second floor apartment looking into an apartment in the next building on the first floor. A girl I knew only slightly was finishing a painting. It consisted of a black arc in the shape of a half circle. I could see blue sky and six men dressed in medieval black suits with large frilly white collars inside the arc. All the men were looking at the arc, each looking at the portion nearest him. I began to pay special attention to the picture, and as I looked closer I noticed the men had clear blue eyes.

I had a special feeling about this dream, and when I was describing it I realized, with a shock, that this painting was not static. Those men were real! Their blue eyes were alive. While I was describing the painting to Jim he suddenly sat upright and listened with a new intensity. And when I was through he asked me to repeat the whole dream again, detail by detail. Jim had read seemingly obscure passages in Jung about the animus, that male dimension of a woman's personality, and how it is often depicted by groups of male figures. Now those figures had stepped off the pages and into my dream. They had become real to both of us. Though it was to be many months before we began to fully understand this dream we sensed its importance. My job was to help finish the painting, to try to complete the circle, and to attempt to get to know the rest of myself. And it was Jung's psychological types that were going to be the chief tool in accomplishing this work.

So come along and let me describe Jung's types, not so that you will end up knowing what I think about them, or even what Jung had to say, but so you can see if they might be one of your happy chances that can help you begin to track the hidden parts of yourself and see into your own life more deeply.

WHAT IS A TYPE?

Even though it doesn't bother us to talk about types of roses or pine trees or human blood, there is something in the very idea of typing people that makes us feel uneasy. Types threaten us from two directions. First, we are afraid that they will pigeon-hole us, deny our uniqueness, and replace it with a superficial label. Secondly, we feel they are somehow undemocratic and could lead to prejudice and repression.

Typology is the study of human differences. C.G. Jung's psychological types are not based on set descriptions that real people must be fit into, but on basic elements which, when combined together, can be used to describe the differences among people. A type is a group of characteristics that stands midway between the universal traits common to us all and those which are uniquely our own. For example, we all have eyes. Yet our own eyes are unlike anyone else's. But between these two poles there are groupings of blue-eyed people, brown-eyed people, etc. Types are a bridge between the universal and the particular. Every typology can be abused in order to deny the universal or the unique in man, but a good typology is a powerful aid to a deeper understanding of who we are.

WHO WAS C.G. JUNG?

C.G. Jung, 1875-1961, was a Swiss psychiatrist and psychologist. He was an early collaborator with Freud, a prolific writer whose collected works fill 18 volumes and the founder of a distinctive school of psychological thought that is being continued and developed today by a world-wide network of Jungian analysts and sympathizers.

But more important, Jung was an intrepid explorer of the inner world of the psyche. For him this inner world, which he called the unconscious, was not simply a basement filled with forgotten memories and useless junk, but was like an ocean or forest filled with beauty and danger, life and death, and meaningful discovery. It was out of his confrontation with the unconscious, both in himself and in his patients, that he slowly elaborated his psychology. His book **Psychological Types** acted as a compass or surveying tool by which he tried to understand how he differed from Freud and Adler, but more importantly, could begin to chart this world within.

THE BASIC ELEMENTS

Our first step in understanding Jung's typology is

to take a quick look at its basic elements, the first two of which are extraversion and introversion. The extravert is someone whose energy and attention is directed outward to the people and things in the world around him, and those objects are decisive in the adaptation he makes and the actions he takes. For the extravert, the world around him is the real world and he adapts himself to it. His own inner world is less real to him and a secondary influence on his conduct.

In contrast, the introvert's energy and attention are directed inwardly. His own inner world is the real world which he adapts himself to and which determines his behavior. He strives to protect this inner world from too strong an influence from the outer world. This outer world is less real for him and therefore of less influence than the inner world. Extraversion and introversion form a pair of opposite basic attitudes to life. Each of us is both extraverted and introverted, for we relate both to the world around us and the world within, but we tend to favor one attitude over the other.

At first I had difficulty distinguishing between introversion and extraversion. I didn't know which one was stronger in me. And then I thought of my mother. She agreed with what the majority thought. She took great pains to look good, say the right things, and do the right things. She sincerely reflected the world around her. If someone disagreed with the generally accepted attitude she would become annoyed at them. Her greatest need was to maintain social rapport. If someone wanted to make waves, or swim upstream, she was displeased. Arguments were not to be settled, they were to be smoothed over in order to preserve social harmony. She wanted everyone to be happy and she bent over backwards to smoothe out wrinkles between people. She was, I saw now, clearly an extravert.

My father, on the other hand, kept his feelings

to himself. He went quietly about his affairs and concentrated on supporting us. He was reserved, and though he would to go parties and dances with my mother, he didn't feel comfortable at them like she did. It seemed he was an introvert. But the real question was, what was I? I had always felt close to my mother, but we would have periodic tussles over my clothes, which I was more or less indifferent to, or how I should be more social, get out more, join clubs, talk more, and so forth. And she had a lot of help in her personal campaign to socialize her backward daughter in the numerous magazine articles that continually appear about how the shy teenager could learn to be the life of the party. I more or less assumed I was extraverted, for my own image of an introvert was tainted by an extraverted society's definition: moody, unsocial, ill-adapted, and melancholic. And I certainly didn't want to be any of those things. But then I started adding up the clues that existed in my own life, and suddenly it clicked. I was an introvert, not according to society's definition, but according to Jung's. I knew that my very first consideration was checking out what was going on inside me. No matter what someone said or did, I would take that experience into myself and decide whether I liked it or not.

Discovering I was an introvert was a psychological revelation. All of a sudden many of the questions that had filled all those years of being a child and a young adult began to disappear. That's why I never felt at ease at parties, that's why I never paid much attention to clothes, that's why I loved spending hours in my room reading, etc., etc. I was no longer such a mystery to myself. Best of all, I knew it was all right to be an introvert. Society's definitions of the morbid melancholic had nothing to do with me. I was happy as an introvert, and greatly relieved that I no longer had to carry the guilt that I would never be a group leader or could never get it together enough to buy a smashing wardrobe. My interests simply didn't lie in those directions, but they did lie in others, which I was now free to explore. I was predominantly introverted, but I knew I had an extraverted side to myself, as well, that came out especially when I was visiting, or entertaining, and in many other activities. But it took a lot of energy to use this extraverted side, surely more energy than the extraverts would ever realize.

No one is only extraverted or introverted, but one side usually predominates. Here is a self-discovery quiz for introversion and extraversion. It's no scientifically formulated test, but simply a way to help you focus on what they mean. So don't worry about what your score on either side is, but try to answer the question of which side is more developed and more your habitual way of relating.

	Introversion	Extraversion
When speaking to strangers I	___sometimes hesitate	___find it quite easy
When I am in a new group I tend more to	___listen	___talk
People would call me	___quiet and reserved	___open and easy to know
When learning about a new subject I like to	___read about it	___hear about it
When it comes to money I am inclined to	___save	___spend

When planning a   ____four people   ____twelve people
dinner I prefer
having

Now try to decide whether you are more introverted or extraverted.

Knowing I was an introvert gave me confidence that I could understand what Jung meant by the four functions which describe the different kinds of introversion and extraversion. These Jung called thinking, feeling, sensation and intuition.

He paired sensation and intuition together as two opposite ways of perceiving. Sensation is the perception of the immediate and tangible reality around us by way of seeing, hearing, touching, etc., and as such is familiar to us. Intuition is also a perception, but of what is in the background, i.e., hidden possibilities and implications. It is similar to the way we understand inspirations and hunches. We perceive something but we are not aware of how we got to that perception.

Thinking and feeling go together as a pair of opposite ways of making judgments. Thinking is the way of judging about the nature of things by means of our ideas and their organization. It concerns itself with the question of truth of falsity. It is not to be confused with intelligence. For Jung, feeling is limited to a sense of rapport or lack of it by which we decide whether we like or dislike something, feel it is good or bad. It is not to be confused with having emotion.

Jung summarized the 4 functions like this:

"Sensation (i.e., sense perception) tells you that something exists; thinking tells you what it is; feeling tells you whether it is agreeable or not; and intuition tells you whence it comes and where it is going."

My next problem was to figure out which of these functions was stronger in me. Just like introversion

and extraversion, I first had to overcome the conno-
tation these words have taken in our society. The
word thinking meant someone who could proceed logically, never got flustered, always knew how to analyze a problem, and was, above all, rational. Feelings, on the other hand, meant something unstable,
something you didn't have much control over, something that couldn't be analyzed. They washed over
you. Feelings meant emotions, both good and bad.

But Jung didn't mean that. For him thinking and
feeling were both equally valid, and were alternative
ways of making judgments. Once some of the stigma
had been removed from the word feeling it allowed
me to realize that I used feeling more than thinking.
I would take my feelings about people or things into myself and know, in no uncertain terms, whether
I liked that person or situation, and I would act on
that judgment. If I say, "I like it because it feels
right to me", thinking types might throw up their
hands in exasperation. But they can't see inside me
where I have put the person or situation on my special feeling scale, and have seen clearly whether it
is good for me or not. They expect that all judgments should proceed by the kind of analysis that
takes place in thinking, where things are divided and
compared and reconnected and a final judgment is
arrived at. If thinking compares one thought with
another in order to advance to a new idea, feeling
weighs the situation and compares it to others. But
it cannot spell out exactly where the final decision
of like or dislike comes from because feeling is more
wholistic than thinking.

In our society thinking is usually considered far
superior to feeling. We put such a high premium on
the verbal analysis of things that we downgrade feeling because it is relatively inarticulate. Who wants
to be a feeler if it somehow means being dumb or
being a second-class citizen who can't really handle
the important jobs in our society? But being a

feeler, according to Jung's terms, has nothing negative about it. Try this next quiz to see if you are more of a thinker or a feeler. Remember you use both, but which one is your habitual way of proceeding?

	Thinking	Feeling
People would consider me	___reasonable	___warm and sympathetic
When people argue I want them to	___come up with a solution	___stop
When someone has a problem my first reaction is to	___help them work it out	___sympathize
When it comes to making a decision I favor	___my head	___my heart

Do you use thinking or feeling more?

My next decision was whether I used intuition or sensation more. For me this was harder. We live in a concrete world. We eat, sleep, go to work, and are surrounded by colors and textures. Our world is physical and we use our senses all the time just to get through the day, and so it was natural for me to assume that I used sensation more than intuition.

But little by little I began to realize it wasn't quite that simple. I really wasn't very good at sensation. Details of my environment escaped me. I didn't notice the clothes people were wearing, for instance, nor could I remember immediately what I had had for dinner last night. I managed to get through my

daily routine, but the physical objects around me did
not capture my attention. Or I might feel tired, and
it wasn't until I ate something - and felt better -
that I would realize what the problem had been.

But what was intuition? It wasn't concrete like
sensation. It was a hunch, a way of sniffing out
possibilities. It wasn't geared to the present like
sensation is, but to the future. Intuition sees what
isn't there yet, but could be. Once I understood
intuition in this way I began to see how often I used
it. When I met someone, it was not the present
moment that counted, or what we were actually
doing, but the possibilities that that relationship
offered. I would dream up a new plan, and then be
impatient with both myself and the project because
it didn't get done fast enough. Today was O.K., but
tomorrow, always tomorrow, would be better. Try the
quiz on sensation and intuition and see which one of
these functions is stronger in you. Again, you have
both, but one is stronger.

	Intuition	Sensation
I tend to	___get excited about the future	___savor the present moment
When I have set plans	___I feel some-what tied down	___I am comfor-table with them
If I were to work for a manufac-turer I would prefer	___research and design	___production and distribu-tion
I am inclined to	___get involved in many pro-jects at once	___do one thing at a time

If people were to complain about me they would say	___I have my head in the clouds	___I am in a rut
People would call me	___imaginative	___realistic
When I find myself in a new situation I am more interested in	___what could happen	___what is happening

Do you favor intuition or sensation?

It had taken me a long time to discover that I favored introversion, feeling and intuition, and now I had one more task to do in order to complete my personal typological picture. I had to fit them all together. Jung had explained that both sensation and intuition, and thinking and feeling, formed pairs of functions that excluded each other. Our conscious function with its attitude tends to push its opposite deep into the other part of the personality. Therefore, someone strongly developed in extraverted sensation would be weakest in the area of introverted intuition. Or someone strongly developed in introverted thinking would be weakest in the area of extraverted feeling.

Well, I knew I favored introverted feeling and introverted intuition, but which one of them was strongest in me? For months I thought it was introverted feeling, which would make my weakest function extraverted thinking. But that didn't fit quite right. I learned more about types and about myself, and finally, one day, it all clicked into place. My strongest function was introverted intuition, and the next strongest, introverted feeling. Following Jung's rule of opposites, this made my weakest area extraverted sensation and my next weakest extraverted thinking.

Are you ready to decide which of the two functions that you chose as more developed is the most developed? Don't be surprised if it is not immediately clear. You can read about types and sometimes you can even make a shrewd guess about what type you are, but that is only the beginning. Psychological types was the way Jung began to look at what he later called the process of individuation. It's not just names and labels we put on ourselves and others, but it is a way of seeing that invites us to work towards our own greater psychic wholeness and to unravel the mixed messages and projections that bedevil so many of the important relationships in our lives. We have to take types out of the realm of words and pure theories and see how they stand up in practice. We have to scruff them up, run them around the block, take them on the freeway and in the office. Types are a tool, and tools are no good if they are not used.

I discovered that one of the best ways for me to learn about my most developed function was to think about my least developed one. Where was I weakest? What situations drove me up the wall? Thinking about these kinds of things is not really fun, but it can be very fruitful. For instance, I had a deep aversion to laundromats. It was a problem for me to organize myself to collect the clothes. I worried about not having the correct change, or enough of it. I was afraid I would forget the soap and would have to go to a supermarket and buy some, and then my greatest concern was that the machine I was using would spill over or would just not work at all, meaning I would have to start all over again with another machine, would lose the money I put in the first one, and I would be delayed an extra half hour in a noisy, mechanical environment. Pure torture. On top of it all, I was afraid someone might steal my clean clothes! Silly, right? Who in their right mind would hate laundromats? But there I was with a real feeling of being tormented. So in my attempt to try to decide which of my functions was my weakest, my laundromat feelings were a good first clue. To wash clothes is to deal with concrete (sensating) things: clothes, money, soap, machines and possible thieves.

Few people who go to laundromats feel like I do, even if they are my own type, or they might share my feelings and be another type. But for me I had an important first clue, and looked around for another one. And I found it in food.

I can cook regular meals, but I find it really hard to dream up a new concoction. I read new recipes, imagine how good they will taste, and look longingly at the picture of the finished product. But the mere thought of buying new ingredients and experimenting with different cooking techniques defeats me. The new idea flies through my mind as an exciting possibility (from my strong intuition), but its execution which demands attention to all sorts of details to textures, smells and even colors in order to make the new meal turn out well exhausts me just to think about it. I did, indeed, have sensation as my weakest function.

Let's look at the various ways in which the basic elements combine to create the psychological types. There are two possible conscious attitudes, four possible first functions and two possible second functions, making 2x4x2 or 16 basic types. Our descriptions, however, will be based principally on eight psychological types without always taking into account the difference in the second function, as for example the difference between the extraverted sensation feeling type and the extraverted sensation thinking type. This will make the descriptions less complicated, but the difference in the second function is of practical importance when it is a question of the development of each type.

You will not find an exact self-portrait in one of the descriptions of the eight basic psychological types that follow, but what I hope you will see is a sketch you can relate to. I hope you will be able to point to one of them and say, "Yes, I can see myself most in this description. I have my own likes and dislikes, my own personal inclinations and my unique talents, but I lean most in this direction." That description will give you an outline of your own basic, personal track. After that comes what Tom Brown calls dirt time: time to crawl around on your hands and knees and watch what happens to your track after the weather has been at it. The winds of chance, the sun of good fortune, the chill of sadness all effect your type. Once you say, "That track is mine," then you have to fill in all the thousands of details that make your track not just a type, but you.

A CAPSULE SUMMARY OF THE EIGHT TYPES

There are four extraverted types: the extraverted sensation type, the extraverted intuition type, the extraverted thinking type, and the extraverted feeling type. And there are four introverted types: the introverted sensation type, the introverted intuition type, the introverted thinking type and the introverted feeling type. Each type hears his own kind of music.

The extraverted sensation type loves to see, hear, taste, touch and smell the world around them.

The extraverted intuition type is continually searching out new possibilities in the world.

The extraverted thinking type has a plan to carry out.

The extraverted feeling type wants to be in harmony with the world.

The introverted sensation type is captivated by the vibrations that the outside world of the senses sets off within them.

The introverted intuition type is continually searching out new possibilities in the inner world.

The introverted thinking type creates interior worlds of ideas.

The introverted feeling type dives deep into the pool of inner feelings.

The Extraverted Sensation Type

The extraverted sensation types are oriented to the world around them to the degree that it can be sensed. They are firmly grounded in the physical world, which they know intimately. They are attuned to nuances of color and sound, as well as shapes, tastes, textures and the number and placement of objects. They experience things in all their vibrant life and detail. What they eat, where they eat, who they eat with, what chair they sit in, what kind of car they drive and what clothes they wear are all alive to them. When they enter a room they notice how many people are present and what the furnishings are like.

This type is my opposite. My weakest function is their strongest, and my strongest function of introverted intuition is their weakest. Remembering this can help me enjoy being with them in a special way. This type likes to have lots of people around, and they are generous with their affection. A large smile and a big hug is the norm. They are open-hearted, and often open-handed with their money. I avoid restaurants because I hate spending so much money on what I consider to be just the task of eating. But not them. Food is a special joy for them. We stopped to visit a friend, and before I realized what was happening he had called up the local Chinese restaurant and ordered a five-course meal for lunch. It was fantastic! Plate after plate was served, all filled with delectable tidbits giving off tantalizing aromas. Money was no consideration when it came to filling the needs of the social occasion.

They can be excellent story tellers, for they recall all the details and relive them for the benefit of the audience. And they love an audience. The more people around to hear them the better. I, in my introversion, avoid crowds, but they encourage them. In their house you can often find two or three people who just happened to drop by, and who are made to feel welcome with a cup of coffee, a piece of pie, and the feeling there is no need for them to rush off. Extraverted sensation types are in no hurry. They live in the present and what is happening now is the most important thing, while I, as an intuition type, live in the future. The extraverted sensation feeling type is very open with her feelings. If she is sad or upset you know about it right away. She might start to cry over her troubles, and throw her arms around you so you can comfort her, whereas I, in trouble, try to find an unoccupied room and close the door. If her feelings are hurt she is crushed. She instinctively trusts people and likes them, and if someone has done something against her she feels betrayed.

The extraverted sensation thinking type excels in remembering facts and figures, and the extraverted sensation types in general can be good cooks and housebuilders, photographers, craftsmen and business people because they have a firm handle on the tangible. They see the physical job to be done, and they are not distracted by all the other possibilities the situation may present. And if they have developed one of their auxiliary functions they can be very effective in getting the job done.

A friend of mine was the head nurse of the emergency room in a city hospital. I went to visit her there one Saturday night. People came in hurt, upset, scared, and my instinct was to run for the hills. But she absorbed it all with an unshakable calm. "What happened? Let me look. This won't hurt." And then some teenagers brought in their unconscious friend. In a glance she had the story: drug overdose. The teenagers were edgy and wanted to slip away, but in two minutes she had them explaining exactly what their friend had taken, and she was off to administer the proper antidotes.

Extraverted sensation types can be especially good with children. The littler the better. Babies need to be fed, changed, bathed, dressed, burped and tickled. Babies are total sensation, and this type loves to use her energy taking care of them.

The extraverted sensation type who does not make enough use of his second and third functions can overuse his first. Then he tries to sense too much and too many thing and not reflect on what these sensations mean but simply try to go on to new and more intense sensations. He can overeat or over-accumulate or overwork or simply overdo whatever his particular preference is. The people and objects around him begin to be treated as occasions or pretexts for more sensation, and he is so caught up in his sensing that he neglects his inner self.

Even when the second and third functions are being used, there comes a point where this kind of adaptation to life is not fully adequate because the inner self is not getting enough attention. This inner self is best represented by the fourth function of introverted intuition which is the way in which the extraverted sensation type can ask the question, "What is the meaning and purpose of my life?" "Where did I come from and where am I headed?" This kind of questioning tends to be excluded from consciousness because it is too opposed to the first function and its extraverted attitude. Yet it is important because it represents another part of who the extraverted sensation type actually is. If he or she cannot come to terms with this part of himself and tries to ignore it or bury it under a crowd of new sensations, then the introverted intuitive dimension will begin to make itself felt, but in a negative and primitive way. The extraverted sensation type can become prey to negative intuitions of future disasters like accidents happening or conspiracies being hatched.

When the extraverted sensation type is fairly well-balanced the introverted intuition can appear in the form of ghosts, spirits and an interest in the parapsychological. One night, for example, when we were staying with friends, just before bedtime they began to tell ghost stories. They told of spirits they had seen flitting around the house, and they told these stories not as fantasies, but with the same sense of concrete detail they they told all their other stories. It was impressive. When the lights went out we felt the urge to look around to see if we, too, could spot one of these spirits.

But the undeveloped inferior function can also be oppressive. It can continually multiply fears and premonitions of disasters. Life becomes cramped. Every minute the extraverted sensation type turns around there is a new negative possibility confronting him, and so his only remedy is to confine himself to a narrow routine of the safe and tried-and-true. The energy for growth that exists in the personality has become split off from the conscious mind and hems it in on every side.

The Extraverted Intuition Type

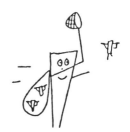

Unlike the extraverted sensation types who are wrapped up in what they are doing at the moment, the extraverted intuition types are future-oriented. The possibilities for tomorrow, next week or next year are what capture their interest. Their energy flows outward, not to the external object but rather around it and through it to the possibilities it suggests. This type takes the physical details that extraverted sensation types linger over and uses them as a spring-board to fly towards what could be. They sparkle with new ideas and plans, many of which have real possibility and merit. They are prolific creators of new businesses, new machines, new social positions and organizations. For the young, healthy extraverted intuition type life is an ever-changing drama with new adventures around every corner. You never know what is going to happen next when you are around them.

When I went with Mike to see his land he had managed to buy in the country, his eyes danced with enthusiasm. Nobody else had even been able to find the land, but Mike had assembled the old maps and searched through the brush to find the old surveying markers. "I'm going to build a house here." He pointed to where a pile of salvaged lumber was stacked. "My well is half dug. It will be wonderful to live back here in the country away from the noise and smell of the city."

But to get an intuition isn't enough. The second function of either thinking or feeling gives the intuition type a way to evaluate his intuitions. For example, the intuition thinking type not only gets the idea for a new business but uses his thinking function to plan out the necessary steps for its establishment, while the intuition feeling type not only sees the possibility of a new social service organization but can bring her feeling function to bear to encourage people to work with her in its establishment.

I love being with this type because they are like me - with a difference. Being extraverted they don't have the same hesitations I do when it comes to dealing with exterior objects and situations. They go up to them and push on through to the other side. Their boldness gives me courage, and while they are at home in the world, they are also constantly changing that world. My intuition is happening inside myself, where no one can see, but the extraverted intuition type is making it happen out there. A new project, a new plan, a new idea not only changes, but hopefully improves the way things are. This type cannot let things alone. There is always a better, or at least another way, and he naturally seeks that new way out.

 But the extraverted intuition types who fail to develop their second and third functions get caught up in more and more intuitions. One follows right on the heels of another, they no sooner try to work one out when another captures their attention, and the end result is that usually nothing gets completely done. Or they conceive one plan and expend enormous amounts of energy establishing it, but just as the goal gets within reach, they get bored with the details, they abandon it and leap head-long into a new adventure. Enough work has been done to satisfy the intuition, but they often don't have the stick-to-it-iveness to finish it. They start one new project after another, oblivious to the reason for the failure of the previous one. They are always sowing

new seeds but hardly ever reaping any of the harvest.

When I saw Mike sometime later still in town, I asked, "When are you going to move out to the new place?" He looked away sheepishly and confessed that he had already sold his house in town and had cleared plenty of money, but instead of using it to work on his land in the country, somehow he had ended up buying a huge abandoned warehouse. Then, in spite of himself, he started getting excited again, telling us how he was going to build a home in the front of the warehouse and then have storage in the back for all his junk cars until he got them fixed, and have a place to build animal pens, and...

And then we come to the difficult fourth function. For this type it is introverted sensation. It is very difficult for him to pay careful and meticulous attention to each detail that goes into the actual execution of his intuition, and it is even more difficult for him to let these sensations slowly soak into him and let himself perceive their implications. For example, he will not stop and listen to the sense impressions of his own body. He becomes so involved in his plans that he forgets to eat lunch. He chases intuitions and works far into the night, forgetting to go to bed. He wears his body down in his race after new intuitions, and his body reacts in the form of accidents or sickness.

Not only his body gives him trouble. The physicalness of objects trips him up, and well. He might want to go on a trip, but he neglects to take care of his vehicle, half-way there he finds himself rolling under the car trying to fix something that he knew all along needed attention, he doesn't have the proper tools with him (he forgot to bring them), he can't do the job, and it usually costs him a lot more in service charges and lost time than if he had attended to the mechanical problem in the first place.

He needs money to keep his plans going, but working full-time, day in and day out at the same job is boring for him. And because his intuition is such a power in him he hates, probably more than any other type, to be told what to do by the boss. He always sees another way to do things.

If something goes wrong, if something breaks down, if he can't accomplish what he set out to do fast enough to satisfy his lightning-quick intuition, he is tempted to rage, kick the vehicle, throw the broken tool across the room, or simply fume and fret. These physical things with their physical problems and limitations impede his marvelous intuitive flow and he wants to punish them.

As this type matures his greatest need is to slow down, make a conscious effort to sit at the table and eat his meals with the family instead of grabbing a piece of bread on the way out the door. He has to pace himself, something he abhors, and it wouldn't hurt to make a schedule of activities and try to follow it. He has to stop and ask the question, "Is the energy and time that is being spent on this intuition worth it to me personally in terms of my own needs, health, family life and social obligations?" Questions like this are hard for the extraverted intuition type to ask because it means pausing to reflect in the midst of his headlong rush after new possibilities.

The Extraverted Feeling Type

The extraverted feeling type lights up a room with the sunshine of her feelings. She wants to be in accord with the world around her. Her feeling rapport with the persons or objects in her environment is her most important driving force. She oils the troubled waters of society and is at the center of its social life. She tends to have many friends of all differents sorts who come to bask in her flow of feeling and sympathy, and go away glad that someone cares about them. She has a knack of focusing her attention on whoever is with her and you can see her visitors open up like flowers after a siege of cloudy weather. They feel like they can let their own feelings out in her presence without the fear of being criticized or ridiculed. They depend on her sympathy and are not disappointed. Since feeling rapport is so important to her she gets upset when people argue. Her goal is to smooth over difficulties and make ruffled feelings go away.

When I am with the extraverted feeling type I am amazed at the ease with which she shows either her sympathy or happiness. I naturally keep my feelings hidden because of my introversion, but hers are on display. It is nothing for her to switch from joy to sadness, depending on what people are telling her. She has no inner journey to travel before the feelings come out like I do. They are up front and accessible to all. When she focuses on me, I can't help but feel happier, or sadder, when I tell her what is going on. She magnifies what I feel.

The second and third functions of either sensation or intuition aid the extraverted feeling type in the accomplishment of this feeling rapport. For example, an extraverted feeling sensation type can make an excellent nurse, or teacher, for she develops a strong relationship to the patient or student and has the ability through the second function to tend to their immediate needs. On the other hand, the extraverted feeling intuition type can be a good social worker who has rapport with her clients and uses her intuition to discover what their real needs are.

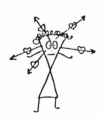

When the extraverted feeling type either has not developed the auxiliary function or has developed them and reaches a state of life where a new kind of adaptation is needed, she can over-use her first function. She can exhaust herself in a whirl of visits, phone calls, shopping trips, and parties, and get so caught up in the succeeding objects of sympathy that she has no time to consider what her own personal opinions and judgments are. She can carry out extensive opinion polls among her many and varied friends as a substitute for making up her own mind.

Her husband had just come through the door, and dinner was almost ready to be put on the table. Judy gave him a big hug - and then the phone rang. It was a girlfriend who wanted to chat. Soon Judy realized the dinner was getting cold, her husband was growing more and more impatient, and still she did not have the heart to cut the conversation short, even though this kind of call ate up her time with him. It took twenty minutes to hang up, and by then not only was the dinner in trouble, she quickly saw she would have to make an extra effort to smoothe her husband's feelings.

Such a predicament is not unusual for this type. They are drawn into the lives of other people, and it is difficult for them to decide when to back off and take time for their own affairs. It takes time, and typological development, to feel free to say "no" to the requests of others.

A fuller adaptation to reality demands the ability to answer the question, "What do I really think?" The greatest weakness of the extraverted feeling type is

introverted thinking, and it is this fourth function that holds the answer to the question of what her personal philosophy of life is. If she ignores this dimension of her personality it does not simply disappear, but it begins to afflict her in the form of negative thoughts about what other people are thinking about her. This begins to effect her rapport with the people around her and she makes social blunders that are inexplicable in terms of her first function. In order to solve the problem of introverted thinking the extraverted feeling type can adopt ready-made philosophies and treat them like her own personal inventions.

The Extraverted Thinking Type

The extraverted thinking type is logical and methodical. It is natural for him to draw on the ideas and facts in the world around him and create a plan from them, or attach himself to an already existing one. Once he has his plan he can be very efficient in carrying out the many operations needed to implement it. If his car breaks down, instead of acting impatient like an extraverted intuition type would, he systematically runs through his mental check list of possible reasons, calmly trouble shoots the problem and repairs it. He sticks with it until it is fixed. This type loves a challenge. Just tell him it is better to stay in bed on a stormy winter morning, and he jumps up and is off to battle the elements.

For the extraverted thinking type the help of the

second or third functions of sensation or intuition gives him the ability to realize what he has thought up. If the second function is sensation, for example, he will have a practical ability to execute his plan here and now. He can be a good mechanic, engineer or executive in charge of day-to-day operations. If intuition is the second function he can be adept at finding innovative ways to carry out his conception.

When I am around this type I know that I will not have to worry about the physical problems that come up when we do a job together. He has control over the situation, he knows what is going on, and he is prepared for possible snags in the operation. The physical world does not threaten him because of his extraversion like it does me as an introvert. But his instinct is to take over. He sees the problem, he decides what to do about it, and that's that. I, as an intuition type, want to explore all the many possible ways of solving it, but he sees only one way, and he doesn't have time to listen to what he considers my flights of fancy.

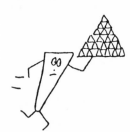

The extraverted thinking type without the aid of the auxiliary functions, or even with their help, reaches a point where his adaptation to reality is too one-sided. He concentrates too intensely on his plans and they act like narrow formulas that squeeze the life out of everything around him and inside him as well. He becomes dogmatic and domineering. Whatever agrees or aids his plan is good, while whatever impedes it is evil, and his way is the only way. When his plan becomes all consuming he will try to walk over anything or anyone who gets in his way. His motto becomes, "Let's get the job done." And he often fails to see the hurt feelings that result.

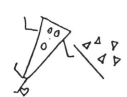

He can become harsh and driven, and neglect his inner self. It is in the area of introverted feeling that this neglect is most severe. He has no time to answer the question, "How do I really feel about myself?" He neglects his health, finances, or personal life in order to try to accomplish his plan, but the introverted feelings will not disappear. His feelings are delicate and he can be hurt surprisingly easily. When his feelings do come out, they take the form of almost childlike sentimentality. A little puppy, a flower, an especially tender story, can bring a quaver to his voice or tears to his eyes. Or they can show themselves in an outburst of ranting and raging.

INTROVERSION

The introverted types are more difficult to describe than the extraverted ones. Extraverts are out in broad daylight doing what they do in the plain sight of everyone, but the flow of energy of the introverts is inward, so their positive qualities are hidden.

We live in a society that is more extraverted than introverted. It is hard to shake the idea that introverts are really undeveloped extraverts. If only, we imagine, they would take an assertiveness training course, get over their shyness, and try to be more social, then they would be all right. Not as good as real extraverts, of course, but they could pass. This bias makes it not only hard for extraverts to understand introverts, but introverts to understand themselves. They can be literally prejudiced against their own natural attitude. Since the introvert's energy travels inwardly first to a world that is as real as the outside world, no matter how hard it is to describe, no one but himself or a few selected people around him see the main action. What the world sees is the small amount of energy that comes back out after its interior journey. No wonder it judges the introvert as a weak and deficient extravert. Let's look, then, at the different kinds of introverts and try to gain a new appreciation of just how real their inner worlds are.

The Introverted Sensation Type

The introverted sensation type is captivated not by the sense object, like the extraverted sensation type is, but by the subjective sense impressions that this object awakens in him. The reverberation and repercussions of the object on his inner world are what his attention focuses on. It is as if a pebble has been thrown into a pond and the ripples spread out throughout the whole inner world of subjectivity, revealing not so much the qualities of the pebble but those of the water it has been thrown in. The sense impressions of this type have a different quality. They are not matter-of-fact like those of the extravert, but have overtones of myth, fantasy and deeper subjective values. The introverted sensation type takes what his senses tell him, brings those details into his inner world, weighs them, experiences them in the depth of his inner self, and only after this process has been completed does the world see an outward reaction.

When I see a friend who is this type and say, "Hi", he looks like he is not reacting at all. He stands there looking blank, but a moment later he greets me. What was happening? Why the lag? He was literally taking in the details of the situation.

My presence had to be absorbed and only when his inner world became saturated with those impressions could he give an outward, delayed and extraverted response to my greeting. Once that initial lag is over our conversation runs smoothly.

Because external stimuli have such an impact on him the introverted sensation type needs to keep his house, office or wherever he spends his time orderly. Neatness is important to his inner psychic comfort. He is uncomfortable in crowds, first because he is introverted, and second because he literally can become overwhelmed by external stimuli if there is too much of it. He needs to know where things are. He also takes very good care of the possessions he has. He values them, not just for what they are as an extraverted sensation type would, but for the added emotional import they have for him. The cherished Christmas tree decorations that have been in the family for years are carefully wrapped in tissue paper and gently placed in a sturdy box until next year. The piece of jewelry given by a loved one is stored in the same velvet-lined box it came in, the love letters have a clean and pressed ribbon around them, and the scribbles of their now-grown three-year-old are saved in a trunk.

The second and third functions of thinking and feeling help organize and evaluate sense impressions. The introverted sensation type can put a great deal of time on one physical project. Unlike the extraverted intuition type who will get bored or impatient, he keeps at it for months, and he excels where attention to detail and order is important, whether it is the repair of delicate machines, the mastering of complicated inventories or making an especially intricate quilt, sewn and embroidered with infinite care. If they choose to build a house the results will be perfect. Each wall, each board, will be carefully measured, skillfully painted, meticulously leveled and plumbed, but it will take him an age. Why? Because each step in the process is not simply done, but is weighed and balanced against the inner image he has inside himself. He might seem slow until you consider the wealth of images and inner sensations he is carrying around and has to sort through. This type makes dinner a quiet ceremony, serves each course with special care, a cup of coffee shared with a friend is not simply a cup of coffee, it is an event, a unique time graced by a beautiful tray and the plate of carefully arranged cookies.

Once when I went to visit a friend, he was fixing his car. If he had been an extravert he would have had a bunch of tools within easy reach, but he had them all lined up, neatly, in a row. If he had been an intuition type he would have had tools thrown here and there, and he would have been missing some, but they were all there. He had carefully collected them for the exact job he was about to do. He took out the part, carefully cleaned it, made sure all the gaskets were dirt-free, and then he just as carefully put the pieces back together again. But remember, first each piece had to travel within and then come out. When I came by I interrupted his peace, quiet and concentration which was essential for the job. He neither wanted, nor could handle, any extra stimuli. The job was his whole world at the moment. When he saw I wasn't going to go away he gave a quiet sigh and reluctantly turned his back on what he was doing, and then I was his one focus. Later he would pick up where he left off and begin again his interior-exterior dialogue with his engine. The extraverted thinker might do the same repair work, and with something of the same thoroughness, but it would be much more matter-of-fact, it wouldn't matter to him how many people were hanging around, and he wouldn't have to take interior trips as he did it.

The weakest function of this type is extraverted intuition, which is why he or she hates change. To move to another house, to get another job, to go to another part of the country, is traumatic. He has absorbed all the details of his present situation and is comfortable with them. To make a physical move is to throw what he has come to feel comfortable with out of the window, and he feels he has to start all over again, meaning he has to take all the thousands of new details, one by one, bring them into his inner world, find a place for them there, and then pick up the next stimulus and repeat the process. Seen in this light we can understand what an upset such a move is for him. A Safeway store in one town is not the same as a Safeway store in another. It is a whole new experience.

The introverted sensation type is slow to make friends. You have to approach them gradually and let them get used to you. It is peaceful for me to be around this type because topics are going to be taken up, one at a time, without a rush. When I am with the extraverted intuition type I have a hard time keeping up with all their ideas, but I find I have to tone myself down when I am with an introverted sensation type. Too many comments or stories tire them out.

The Introverted Intuition Type

The introverted intuition type gazes inward, not to the ripples of sensation caused by the object like the introverted sensation type, but beyond these palpable facts to try to see their root and meaning. They are visionaries par excellence, seers and dream-

ers. They are caught up in the explorations of the inner world and the possibilities of inner transformation. They can follow these inner paths by way of images and ideas, and they are always attempting to go deeper and find the ultimate origin and goal of the inner self.

The introverted intuition type is not concerned with what is, but what could be, not with the outer possibilities, but the inner ones. They can have a special love of books, for books let their minds go anywhere while they are comfortably curled up in their own room. One intuition triggers another as they leap through the centuries and soon they are exhausted without ever having moved.

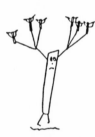

The second and third functions of thinking and feeling help the introverted intuition type in evaluating and organizing these inner journeys, but even then he has difficulty in expressing his interior world because this demands a certain degree of extraversion. His words tend to be fragmentary and evocative, as if he cannot tear his eyes from his inner world long enough to formulate what is happening in everyday language.

The weakest function for this type is extraverted sensation. He might be carried away with his theories, but his socks don't match. He might be taking daily trips through space mentally, but he forgets what he went to the store for. This type finds it difficult to pay attention to the actual here-and-now physical world that the extraverted sensation type is so comfortable in. He inadvertently tends to bump into things, spill things, drop things, have his mind on something other than his food when he eats, and scarcely notices the clothes he wears or the colors of the walls of the rooms in which he lives.

I attended a lecture where the professor bustled into the classroom late, as usual, sat down in the circle of chairs and placed his huge briefcase in front of him. His suit was rumpled and as he got up to search for his pipe, he managed to trip over the briefcase he had just put down. Tobacco began to dribble down his shirt as he waved the pipe in the air while he expounded on the subject of the day. Soon the pipe was forgotten, resting precariously on his knee, from there to slide into the already bulging briefcase. Too bad it hadn't been lit, for it was clear that a fire was the only way the briefcase would ever get cleared out. We students continued to watch, fascinated, as he punctuated his lecture by squirming around in his chair, slowly managing to dislodge his wallet from his pants pocket.

Social situations are not comfortable for him, and the bigger the group the worse it is. He thrives and comes alive when there is just one other person to talk to, but crowds make him uneasy, and he is especially miserable when it comes to small talk. He does not make a good first impression because all the action is going on inside, and he needs a special atmosphere for it to come out.

He loves quiet and solitude, not in the way society thinks of morbid introverts, but simply because it takes peace and quiet in order to go on these interior journeys. It's not enough just to have an idea, he has to push it to see if it will flower into a deeper version of the original concept, or if some new rich vein of intuition will open up to him.

Time is of the utmost importance to the introverted intuition type. He would rather eat peanut butter crackers in a low-rent apartment than go out to expensive restaurants and have a fancy house as long as the former means time for his own interests and the latter demands a full-time job doing what someone else wants him to do. Introverted intuition types flourish where bold speculation comes into its own in research and theoretical science. But since they are the most ill-adapted of all the types to the real physical world they run the danger of losing touch with ordinary life. When the introverted intuition type neglects extraverted sensation, he is not simply excused from it. He can become subject to obsessions, compulsions and scruples about food or sex which are attempts by the extraverted sensation part of the personality to gain his attention and receive their due.

The Introverted Feeling Type

The extraverted feeling type attaches her feelings to the people and things around her, but the introverted feeling type tries to be in rapport with her inner world, whether it be of psychic images or ethical and spiritual values, and she tries to intensify this inner accord and embrace this world more deeply and fully. For the introverted feeling type the people and things around her are occasions for her feelings, which flow inward and go deeper and try to become more intense and concentrated.

Because of the direction of her feelings she is often accused of not having any. She has a feeling, then that feeling immediately travels to her inner world, she weighs it on her interior feeling scale, and only once the round-trip journey has been made can she express herself. So much inner activity is going on that she tends to keep her face and body still. People often overlook this type, or are quick to classify her as slow. If we could have an exterior picture of what is really going on, however, we would be astounded. She lacks spontaneity not only because she is an introvert, but because her feelings are a constant involvement for her.

It was a peaceful afternoon and a neighbor came over to chat with Betty and her mother. She casually mentioned that a neighborhood dog (the one Betty had spent hours with in happy contentment) had died. Betty froze. Her heart felt as though it had been pierced, but she showed no outward sign of her inner turmoil. At long length the neighbor ambled off, Betty rushed into the house, and in the solitude of her own room, she broke out into racking sobs. Her beloved friend was gone.

The introverted feeling type tries to protect herself against too strong an influence coming from the outer object and detach her feelings from it so that they can travel within. Her clinging to inner values, silent as it is, can provide a good example from an ethical and moral point of view. People around her sometimes sense this inner reality, and fidelity to inner values. But at other times they sense how they are somehow being treated with a certain reserve, held in check and subtly devalued.

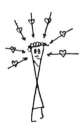

The second and third functions of sensation and intuition can help her perceive her inner values. Her third, more extraverted function helps her come to grips with the outside world. The introverted feeling types can be literally bursting with feelings but have no ready way to communicate them both because of their direction and because their content is not readily explicable in everyday terms.

Extraverted thinking is her weakest function. If she has a conversation, for example, she might spend hours, or even days, still thinking up answers she could have given but didn't. Though she might really care for someone, that person might remain in the dark because she cannot express herself well.

She is easily tripped up by a thinking type who overpowers her with his words. When this happens she gets overwhelmed and can no longer respond. If you show displeasure or impatience with her, she is totally lost and her introverted feelings block up her weak thinking power, and she can easily be made to feel inadequate in our more verbal, active society. When upset, she will give you dark looks but it might be days before you know what is bothering her. Her fourth function thoughts are like birds - they come and go, and often fly off before they can be caught.

The Introverted Thinking Type

While the extraverted thinking type starts with facts and ideas he finds in the world around him and ends up with plans to be accomplished, the introverted thinking type makes facts serve his thoughts. He uses them to help build his inner world of ideas. He takes delight in pursuing the orderly development of his own ideas until he has created a logical kingdom within.

His outer conduct often reflects this inner sense

of order. He can be organized, make a plan for the day, and actually follow through on it.

Once when we spent the day with a friend of this type it was a fascinating and enjoyable experience of precision planning. It started with a well-balanced breakfast for the whole family that he cooked and served with a minimum of fuss. Then off we went for a guided tour of all the local attractions carefully selected in advance to appeal to all the different members of the family.

The auxiliary functions of sensing or intuition help him develop this interior world of thought. If intuition dominates he may devote his energy to philosophy or law or theoretical science. If sensation is the companion to thinking, he can be attracted to accounting or business.

If he concentrates excessively on his own world of thought he will begin to neglect the rest of life that can't be expressed in thoughts. He will be tempted to say, "If I can't think it, it isn't real." Then the thoughts begin to imprison him and can even lose their objective character, for they become substitutes for developing the rest of his personality.

The greatest weakness of the introverted thinking type is in the area of extraverted feeling. He has difficulty in expressing his feelings, and when his feelings do come out, other people are not always comfortable with them. He gives the appearance of lacking compassion, and is inclined to say things that others take as sarcastic or insulting. But he doesn't see them that way. He feels he is just trying to be logical. He gains a reputation for being self-contained, competent and even cold. But he has feelings, and plenty of them. It's just that they are deep down, hard for him to express, and delicate and easily hurt when they come out.

What Is Your Psychological Type?

As I mentioned, it took me a long time to finally figure out what type I was. You will probably be quicker, but don't become impatient with yourself. The more your appreciation of your own type takes into account the memories, dreams, fantasies, and experiences that go to make up you, the more useful your final decision will be.

No quiz, no matter how artfully constructed, can replace this slow process of type recognition. It is hard to convey what this kind of tracking is like. It would be much easier if we could go tracking together and evaluate real life situations. Then we could see the tell-tale hesitation that marks an introvert when he meets someone for the first time, or the enthusiasm that fills an extraverted intuition type when he is in the grip of a new idea. Or we could walk down one of those difficult type trails where we accumulate clues, each one of which is like a knotted thread on the back of a tapestry. And then after months, or even years, after endless revisions and reevaluations, we would see these perceptions finally come together. The tapestry is suddenly flipped over, and in a moment we understand that person's type.

CHAPTER 2

TYPE DEVELOPMENT

The best possible result of working your way through the last chapter is that you have discovered your own type, or at least the direction in which to look for it. This discovery, though it is the end of one process, is just the beginning of another. The knowledge of our own type is simply the key that opens the door to the adventure of typological development. Types are dynamic. We have to develop within ourselves and grow in relationship to the people around us, and the inside and outside work go hand in hand. The more we know our own type the more clearly we can see others, and the more clearly we can see them the better chance we have of being objective about ourselves.

But working with types is not a parlor game. When people say something like that I can only shake my head in wonder. I was going through mental struggles trying to figure out my own type, and my discoveries, rather than boxing me in, were showing me possibilities for my own personal growth that I had never been aware of. They were a tool with which I could look at myself, not only now, but what I had been like as a child and what sort of possibilities were open to me in the future. Types were not caging me in like an exotic bird with a fancy name, but opening the door of the cage that I had literally been in all my life because I had had little idea of what I was really like.

Types are an important tool for inner growth. But their dynamic nature demands respect. Who would have much sympathy for us if we ran off to the woods with a brand new chain saw and no experi-

ence, and tried to fall towering trees? Types begin
to open the door to the unconscious and release some
of the powerful energies that dwell there. It is these
energies that deepen and reshape our personalities.
It would be ideal if we always had some knowledge-
able guide to turn to, a Jung or a typological Tom
Brown. But unfortunately life does not always provide
us with these opportunities. So work with someone
you trust if you can, but if you have to go forward
on your own, open this door bit by bit and gradually
test the waters of the unconscious.

Let me tell you what happened to me. My dream
had shown me the work I had to do, and Jung's types
had provided me with a tool to do it. But what I
didn't realize was how painful and difficult it was
going to be to get in touch with my other half that
the dream had portrayed.

My dream should have given me pause. Why was
the girl who was doing the painting in another building? Just where was the other half of the personality? My other side wasn't just waiting there for me
to finally wake up and recognize it so that by that
simple fact alone we could live happily ever after.
Once I had a clue to what my own type was, it had
been natural for me to try to see my type in the
concrete by examining how I had developed typologically. I reached back to my earliest memories and
tried to see in them my particular type in embryonic
form and how it had been molded and shaped over
the years. What began to emerge was a very different picture of my own type. I was seeing what Jung
had said, but now in the concrete through my
memories and dreams. I was on an actual journey,
or safari, to the other side.

Slowly I began to see that my two sides were
split. It was as if they were polarized in different
directions, and sometimes were even antagonistic. I
began to realize that the types of my parents had
deeply imprinted themselves on me. Whatever splits

and tensions had existed in their personalities and whatever difficulties that existed in their marriage had twisted and pulled at the wax of my own type.

It wasn't enough to know some type theory, and now I saw it wasn't even going to be enough to see in concrete detail what type I was. These splits and polarizations inside myself were loaded with energy. In fact, the very energy I needed to grow and fulfill the promise of my initial dream was fixated there, and I had to somehow go down into myself and release it. The way I did it was something I ended up calling feeling sessions. I would recall a memory that evoked strong feelings in me, relive it in my imagination, and allow all those feelings to become fully alive again as if the event were happening today.

A memory: A girlfriend invited me to a party, and I was thrilled at the prospect of meeting new boys. When I got there, though, I quickly saw that the boys already knew most of the girls, and they quickly paired off, leaving me to fret in a corner. What I had envisioned as being romantic and exciting became pure torture. I was filled with frustration, anger, and self-loathing. Why couldn't I be popular, too? What was wrong with me? Why didn't anyone pay any attention to me? The hours dragged by as I methodically tore a ping-pong ball to shreds.

When I recalled that memory I let all those feelings wash over me. Once more I was the insecure teenager who craved attention. Once more I felt trapped. Once more I felt myself whither up and die inside myself. Once more I pictured the couples dancing, or in dark corners kissing. Once more I felt inadequate and ugly. I made an effort to forget nothing. The palms of my hands once more broke out in sweat, and the misery overcame me. I cried over that night, even though it had happened ten years before.

But to remember it in all its agony wasn't enough. I would replay it over and over again, and

each time the force of those emotions would diminish. If I had simply analyzed the memory without
letting the hurt and anguish come out into the clear
light of day, it would have done me no psychological
good. It was only once those feelings were alive
again that I could work with them. It was only in
the reality of the emotional experience that I could
then analyze it in terms of type. But first I had to
lance the wound and release the unresolved suffering
that I had conveniently forgotten and put deep down
where I thought it could no longer hurt me. But as
long as I refused to reflect on that memory it would
still have power over my today. Once the full force
of those feelings were again alive and allowed to
diminish naturally through the continual replay of it,
only then could I see just why I suffered so. Only
then could I explain to myself that my introversion
had frozen me in an extraverted situation surrounded
by strangers. Only then could I realize the conflicts
I felt about meeting new boys in the first place
because of my shaky relationship with my own third
function of thinking. Only then could I begin to come
to terms with my own conflicts with the outer world
because of my introversion. The end result was that
memory no longer was an unrecognized cause of
pain. I had taken the feelings, released them and
coupled them to my typological understanding, and
this vibrant combination was the alchemy necessary
for a small step toward growth.

What I did with my memories I did with my
dreams, as well, by reliving the feelings that the
dream images evoked. And so it went, day after day,
week after week. I had never realized there was so
much pain inside myself. But all this work was opening up new parts of me, building bridges, and letting
the waters of life in my psyche flow. And the resentments and fears that were now being transformed
into creative energies allowed love to bubble up as
well, not only for myself as a unique individual, but

for my parents and all those that had been bound up in my past. And I told all these things to Jim in detail. Neither one of us had realized what was in store when I had had that first dream. We were discovering what typology had really meant to Jung. It was a powerful way in which to enter into the process of individuation. Looking back I see that we ran all sorts of risks by going on that journey into the unconscious. We knew so little, and the energies were so powerful. It was as if we were in a little boat on the ocean and waves were threatening to swamp us. But there was no going back. We had to try to reach the other shore.

I am honestly not sure what to say when I see someone who could benefit from this kind of psychological work. I could say that everyone ought to go to a Jungian analyst who will help them on this night sea journey. But analysts are few and far between, and often we need the help types could give us in our marriage or family life or in becoming who we were meant to be. But types have an inner tendency to lead us into the journey of individuation. And that journey is a difficult and serious business. You will have to decide for yourself how deeply to get involved in it.

Let's start this journey of type development by looking briefly at how dreams, daydreams and moments of high feeling can be understood typologically.

1. Dreams. Dreams are graphic pictures of what the other side of our personality is like. They tend to compensate for our conscious one-sidedness and so if we pay attention to them they can give us a living picture of the struggle between conscious and unconscious, and the dominant and the least developed function. In them a drama is being played out which has to do with our instinctive urge to be whole and complete, and if we can understand the charac-

ters we can take a more decisive role in helping this
process along. The more dreams in a series we possess, the more chance we have of finding clues in
one dream that will help unravel another. One way
which we can interpret dreams is from the perspective of our own type and how it is growing, and the
problems it is facing.

Tom, an introverted intuition type
    Dream: Tom was in the back seat of a car and
there was a strange man who was driving fast and
somewhat recklessly. Tom's girlfriend was in the
front passenger seat, and sometimes she would turn
around and hold Tom's hand, but at other times she
flirted with the driver. Tom woke up with a feeling
of anxiety about the possibility of losing his girlfriend. The strange man reminded him of the foreman
on his last summer job whom Tom felt was coarse
and loud.
    Interpretation: The strange man symbolizes Tom's
extraverted sensation function which is a stranger to
consciousness and not particularly reliable. In contrast
to Tom's conscious life which is directed by intuition, the dream shows the other side where the sensation function is in the driver's seat. The girlfriend
can be understood as a symbol of Tom's third function, feeling, which is pulled in two directions: on
the one side towards the consciousness represented
by Tom, and on the other towards the stranger. The
feeling function is partially conscious and partially
unconscious.

    2. Daydreams. If we have recurrent daydreams and
fantasies we can try to interpret them in the same
fashion, for they are filled with material from the
other side of our personality.
    Daydream: Tom had a recurrent fantasy about
being in a plane crash in a remote place. The crash
had left the passengers with hardly any supplies and

no ready means of help. It was Tom, drawing on his interior resources, who organized shelter using branches and leaves, found edible plants and took charge of the survival of the group. In the process of doing this, the most beautiful woman among the passengers was drawn to him because of his command of the situation.

Interpretation: The weakest part of Tom's personality is in the area of extraverted sensation. The daydream indicates that the function of intuition symbolized by the plane is no longer adequate. The unconscious, by means of the daydream, presents to him another Tom who is strong in this area and reaps the rewards of his strength. These images, coming from the unconscious, attempt to compensate for the one-sidedness of the conscious, and can be seen as an attempt to attract Tom to further self-development.

3. The Analysis of Moments of High Feeling Intensity. There are events in our lives that seem to strike us much more intensely than warranted by the actual facts of what happened. They are loaded with an extra charge of energy which comes not from the event itself but from the unconscious. The event has hit something there and released some of the energy the unconscious has, and the result is some kind of upset, depression or elation. If we can discover what it is in the other side that is so energy-filled, we will get a new insight into what our other side is like.

A Moment of High Feeling Intensity: One day Tom was paging through a magazine and he read a short anecdote about a man who had spent 30 years in a mental hospital. The man had stated that the most fulfilling thing that had happened to him during all that time was that once, while working on the hospital newsletter, he had won an argument with the staff person in charge of the paper about how a

particular word should be hyphenated. For some reason that Tom couldn't fathom at the time, he
couldn't forget that story.

Interpretation: The story symbolized in Tom's mind
the possibility of being trapped in the world, just like
the mental patient had been locked up in the hospital. As an introverted intuition type, Tom loved freedom and feared that the details of sensation would
tie him down and not let him fly. Tom was concerned about living a meaningful life, and was afraid
that he would be caught in situations where fulfillment and meaning were hard to come by. The patient who had only one apparently trivial moment of
fulfillment in 30 years symbolized Tom's fears.

Tom's understanding of these messages from the
unconscious has to be followed by his active work
in contacting the psychic energy connected with
them, as I did in my feeling sessions.

Now let's turn to how we can learn to see our
relationships with our parents, friends, spouse and
children from a typological point of view.

Types Together

The best preparation for dealing with people of
other types is to have dealt with types within ourselves. If we can see in a personal and practical
manner how we are a community of types with
strengths and weaknesses, we can see other people
more clearly, for they, too, are not simply types but
totalities. I am not only an introverted intuition
type, for instance, but also an introverted feeling
type, an extraverted thinking type, an extraverted
sensation type, in fact all eight types, and so are
you. It is all too easy to succumb to putting a superficial label on our fellow man instead of going
through the hard work of trying to understand him.
Even if this label reads an extraverted intuition type,

or an introverted sensation type, it will not solve our conflicts with others unless we are striving to heal these conflicts within ourselves. This superficial form of characterization always upset Jung, for he felt that it missed the reality of types as an inner dynamic process of individuation. Types can be used to explore relationships, and Jung himself used them in this way in trying to help explain husbands to wives, parents to children, etc., but we have to be continually on our guard against losing sight of the complex realities they represent, and settling simply for the naming of the most conscious function.

Types and Tolerance

If we understand the nature of typology, this fact alone is a big step towards making us more tolerant, even though we are not certain what the other person's type is. The beginning of tolerance comes from the recognition of the existence of legitimate diversities among people. We realize there is the possibility of understanding someone's conduct and we can view it as a task to be accomplished rather than seeing their behavior as an intolerable annoyance. We can realize that we have something in common with the other person, even if it means reaching into the less developed parts of our personality in order to find it, and we can be alert to appreciate his talents because they can help us become stronger.

Types and Stereotypes

We often see the people around us through the colored glasses of our conscious function. Yet we believe that we are being totally objective. Objectivity is a goal we strive towards, but not only is our conscious way of looking at things tinted by our own dominant attitude and function, but the other less developed parts of ourselves are having their say and effecting how we see people without us realizing it.

Though parts of ourselves are unconscious, that does not prevent them from getting us into trouble, and part of their mischief is to make the people around us appear different from the way they actually are. Why does the unconscious do that? Simply because it is trying to find a way to bring itself to our attention, and if we won't look within, it will go outside and approach us from there. This process is called projection. It hovers around the edge of consciousness and forms a subtle atmosphere of prejudgment.

For example, the extravert sees the introvert as painfully shy and socially backward, stuck in himself and unwilling or unable to come out into the healthy sunshine of life. He is melancholic and brooding, preoccupied with self to such a degree that it can lead only to morbidness and dark deeds.

For the introvert the extravert is all bluster and show, a whirlwind of action and talk who tries to hide the fact that there is no substance to him. He is a hollow man, who has given up his soul to run after trifles. He is frivolous or flighty, or worse, overbearing and tyrannical.

The sensation type can feel that the intuition type doesn't have his feet on the ground. He is flying off into a fantasy world at the least provocation while he ignores the most basic facts of life like proper meals, cleanliness, earning a living, and the other realities of living in this world.

The intuition type often sees the sensation type in the guise of a carnal man stuck in his immediate environment and preoccupied with eating, sleeping, dressing and working, all to excess, and whose idea of fun is some dreary repetitive game.

The feeling type looks on the thinking type as a cold inhuman computer who would rather be with numbers, machines or involved ideas than with people. The thinking type appears rigid, uncaring and without heart, and a living time bomb when you do manage to drag him into a social gathering.

For the thinking type the feeling type is above all else unreasonable. She is constantly off on emotional tangents or pestering you to death with her entreaties or complaints, or just plain gushing in a way which is impervious to good sense and a clear statement of position.

The simple recognition of our particular inclinations to prejudice is an important first step in eradicating them. The real process of becoming unprejudiced is in our healing of the splits that exist in our own personality so that they will not be projected outward.

Projection and Prejudice

Projection is all around us and is at the source of many misunderstandings and hatreds. White America has harsh words and contempt for Blacks, Indians, and Mexican Americans. Yet the dreams of the white men are filled with these people, making it quite clear how much of a projection this racial prejudice is. No doubt the projection works both ways. In a similar manner the West loathes the East, the Arabs hate the Jews, the Irish, the English, and on and on without end. The real fire for such hatred is not only in historical events, but in a lack of integration. To the degree we fail to come to grips with the full extent of our own personality, we project the unconscious contents outward on those around us. Those contents, since they have been neglected and starved for attention for so long, can be crude and antagonistic, frightening and bestial, which are precisely the characteristics of the classic enemy - whether it be a Communist, white man, red man or whatever.

There are, of course, good and bad actions of individuals and nations, as well as varying levels of culture and different value systems. But we cannot come to grips with these objective issues until we are aware of our own subjective projections which distort all we see like mirrors in a fun house - or house of horrors.

Types and Environment

From the moment we are conceived we are being molded and shaped by the environment around us. We can imagine the type we are born with to be a particular kind of seed. If we are a lettuce we should not expect to be transformed into a tomato or a cabbage or even another variety of lettuce. But this does not make our environment unimportant. The environment is like the soil we grow in and the water we are given. Environment is vitally important. It determines how the seedling will grow and if it will reach maturity and bear fruit. Good environment can be a question of life and death. Let's look at how our parental environment can shape our type.

Parents

The effect of our parents is so profound that it is only with great difficulty that we can distinguish their influence from our inborn type. It is important to see this influence in order to decide what we really are in ourselves and how we can develop our own true potential. Our parents imprint their types on us with their good traits and positive energies, as well as their weaknesses and fears. This they do simply by being our parents and also by having expectations both voiced and unvoiced about what we should be like. In order to map out their influence we have to know what their types are and then see how they have interacted with our own.

Peter, an extraverted sensation type father, and

Sammy, an introverted intuition type son

It always upset Peter when he would come home from work or be home for the weekend, and there Sammy was in his room, reading a book or playing endlessly with his toy soldiers. "What's the matter with that kid? He is so quiet and has just a few friends, and is always dreaming and tripping over his own feet. How will he ever amount to anything if he doesn't get some get-up-and-go? Why, when I was a kid I played on the Little League ball team, I had dozens of friends, and I had a part-time job after school as well. But I can't really say anything without the wife butting in and defending him. He's just a mama's boy."

Martha, an extraverted feeling type mother, and Annie, an introverted intuition type daughter

Annie, age 10, was coming home from school, and as she approached the house she realized with a sinking feeling that the Bridge Club was having a meeting there. "Oh, no. She'll want me to face all those ladies and say hello." Sure enough, even though Annie tried to escape by running up the stairs without anyone seeing her, her mother's voice, with a slight threat in it, said, "Annie, come and say hello to everyone", and then in a whisper, "And be sure to be nice." "Hello", Annie mumbled to the ladies, and then fled again, this time with success.

George, an introverted thinking type father, and Bob, an extraverted sensation type son

Bob couldn't get his father to understand how important it was to him to join the school's football team. He saw it as the way he could be really popular with his classmates. George, on his part, had never been too interested in group sports, and didn't want to see his son waste a lot of time and energy that could go towards more important things, or have him get hurt.

On the surface, these stories are ordinary, and each of us has dozens of them about our own childhood. What possible value could they have in helping us to have a deep insight into ourselves and our relationship with our parents? Let's take our first example of Peter and Sammy, and explore it further. Little Sammy's type and his father's can be represented as follows:

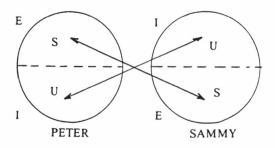

Sammy has a natural weakness in the area of extraverted sensation. This is what is irritating his father to begin with, and his father unwittingly, by making an issue of Sammy's deficiencies, is widening the split between the conscious and the unconscious, or the extraverted sensation part of Sammy's personality and the rest of it. This just aggravates the problem and will make it more difficult for Sammy to cope with his inferior function, both now and in the future. His father can't really appreciate Sammy's gifts either, because they strike him at his weakest point, and he unthinkingly perceives them with an aura of suspicion and even potential danger. We tend to sympathize with little Sammy, but his father is not deliberately trying to make trouble for him, and is himself disappointed because he doesn't have the kind of son he wished for. If both of them understood the typological differences involved, they would have a much better chance for a deeper and more fruitful relationship.

If the basic outline of our type interaction with our parents is clear, we can begin to explore our personal history in regards to them, especially concerning moments that have high feeling energy. Take an event and see if you can explain it in terms of your type and that of your parents. This kind of procedure can actually release all sorts of energy. Use this energy in a positive, constructive fashion to develop your type. There is little use in blaming your parents for what they did or did not do. What were their parents like? The important point is to break the chain of events in yourself so you do not blindly pass on your own problems to those you influence. If your feelings build up too strongly, back off until you can get them under control or release them in private. Go where you can be alone and do some shouting and crying and beating of pillows about what should have been done and how you should have been treated. Then get on with the job of constructive personal change. We can change ourselves but not change others directly, so most face-to-face recriminations about the past are worse than useless. Resist the sometimes almost irresistible tendency to confront your parents with their apparent shortcomings. We can follow the same sort of procedure with our brothers and sisters, childhood friends and teachers, etc., and see how they shaped us in this early formative period.

Types and Children

Children, even from infancy, can show distinctive kinds of behavior which can be understood in terms of types. Many parents have noticed how different their children are even though they grow up in the same home and get the same kind of love and affection. We take far too much upon ourselves if we think that the real and deep-seated differences which we see in our children are only a consequence of our own behavior. Instead we have to realize that we are often dealing with a person of another type, and even if our child is our own type, they are at a different stage of development.

If we adopt a typological perspective we have a good framework in which to understand both the child's strengths and weaknesses. But too often we work on his strengths and ignore or complain about his weaknesses. And in doing so we are imitating what society as a whole does. It has a natural inclination to foster the development of the most differentiated function of the child. This is because a community rates the individual not on their wholeness, but on the distinctive contribution each can make to it. Too often we as parents blindly follow the same pattern. We see that our child has a particular gift, and we go out of our way to cultivate it, whether it is some kind of artistic, intellectual or athletic ability. The unfortunate result can be a child who develops one-sidedly. A child's strengths will tend to come out naturally and we can often devote our time more fruitfully to helping them with the problem represented by their least developed function.

For example, an introverted thinking type boy with a high verbal ability can find enough stimulation for his talents without a special program of development. Where he really needs help is in the area of extraverted feeling so that his conscious growth in introverted thinking does not overshadow and suppress this aspect of his personality. It's wonderful for a mother to be proud of how articulate her son is, but there is no one who is in a better position to draw out his hidden and delicate feelings. The development of the least developed side of the personality of their child is a special and privileged task of parents.

Parents also have a responsibility to monitor the environments in which their child lives outside the home in order to see if there is enough freedom in them for their child's particular kind of developmental needs. There has to be room in the school room, the church activity group, the clubs, and the sports teams for all different types of children. If one model is held up to the exclusion of all others, then many children will be harmed.

The field of adoption is another place where it is important to recognize differences in type. If the couple who wants to adopt a child is aware of their own types and the varying degrees of difficulty with which they deal with other types, they can either look for the type of child that will be compatible with them or be aware that the child, no matter how young they have received it, could have a psychological type very distinct from their own. For example, an extraverted couple has to be aware of the possibility of adopting an introverted child in order that their own expectations will not be disappointed and that the child will not be put at an immediate disadvantage.

Children, even at 8 or 10 years old, and perhaps even before that, can develop a surprisingly good knowledge of type differences. It gives them a framework within which their parents can explain countless situations, and the children themselves can begin to make their own tentative explanations.

In the give-and-take of active family life, if all the members of the family are aware of their inferior function, it makes them more tolerant of each other. The children can distinguish bit by bit the occasions when they are being yelled at due to their own misconduct from those in which they have simply rubbed their parents' inferior function the wrong way, and the parents can learn to admit when they are upset because of their own weaknesses.

Our own children grew up hearing Jim and I talk about types, and they didn't have any trouble catching on to the idea of projection. If I got angry at them, more often than not they would interrupt a

fine rage I had generated and say, "You're projecting, Mom." That has the irritating result of making
me stop in my tracks and consider whether, in fact,
I was projecting on them. Sometimes they were
right, and I found myself in the uncomfortable position of having to apologize. At other times I could
say that no, I was not projecting. They really were
being impossible. In our family not only does a child
recognize a projection, (actually, it's rather easy: my
voice reaches a certain pitch, my face turns red and
I threaten physical violence), he can usually elaborate
on the theme: "You're oversensated," meaning my
weak extraverted sensation is at its limit. But it can
(happily) work the other way, too. I can say to the
child, "Look, I am getting overloaded. Please go away
for a little while before I blow up." And the child
looks at my tense face and wisely decides that it
just might be a good idea to disappear.

Now that the children have entered the teenage
years, we talk more and more about type development. Our son has to work on his third function feeling rather than try to pretend he is all-macho and
doesn't have any, and our daughter struggles with a
weak thinking function, especially when she is faced
with doing math. But now we have the vocabulary
to work out our problems, and a satisfying degree
of typological understanding so that the child can
look inside himself, or relate a particularly disturbing
dream, and know he has work to do on himself. The
frustrations and nameless rebellious feelings no longer
make a victim of the budding teenager. Those very
feelings can be the impetus for important typological
work.

CHAPTER 3

MARRIAGE AND THE FOURTH FUNCTION

In the last two chapters we have covered some of the basics of type recognition and type development, but two of the most important topics remain: types in marriage and the challenge of the fourth function.

At first glance the wonderful and painful experience of falling in love may seem far removed from psychological types, but it isn't. In fact, understanding what falling in love means is one of the best ways to grasp the real meaning of types. When we fall in love we feel a completeness and wholeness deep within ourselves. We are overwhelmed with a feeling of luck and gratitude. It's all too good to be true, and yet it is happening, and we attribute it all to the fact that we have finally found the right person for us.

But if we stop for a moment and look at falling in love from the point of view of types, another picture emerges. As an introverted intuition feeling type, I am comfortable with that introversion, and I feel at ease with my first and second functions, but the other half of my personality, the half that is extraverted, and contains the functions of thinking and sensation, remains buried in my unconscious. But just because I am blind to that half of myself doesn't mean it doesn't make itself felt. I am searching for that other half, but I do it not by looking inside myself, but outward. When I fall in love I am overcome by the feeling that for the first time in my life I am whole. Why? Because you are an extravert, and your first two functions are sensation and thinking. What you are is the mirror image of my unconscious. I cannot see that half of myself, but I can see you, and I am entranced. And you fall in love with me for the same reasons. Together we are perfect. We feel as though we have reached a new level of ecstasy, and we can't bear the thought of being apart.

Falling in love is a special kind of projection. You are my other half, literally, from a psychological point of view, and you are mine. But there is a problem. If I could look at my inner unconscious half, I would see how imperfect, scarred, undeveloped and unruly it is. But by looking only at you I see my own inner half that is free of my own imperfections and splits. It as though the inner half of myself jumped suddenly into the full light of consciousness in wholeness and beauty. So in falling in love with you I am falling in love with the hope and promise that I can be whole and complete.

Unfortunately, we don't understand that there are two processes going on at once. We mistake a promise of wholeness for the actual fact. We think if we could only be together forever our problems would be solved. We make our own sense of completeness depend on the other person. Without being aware of it we have transferred the interior task of our own self-development to our partner. By being with you I no longer have the feeling that I am incomplete within myself, and it is as though, suddenly, by meeting and loving you, I am completely developed, all in an instant.

But even though loving you gives me an intoxicating taste of wholeness, it cannot be the instant cure for my own imperfections and weaknesses. There is no short-cut to wholeness. There is no way to avoid the difficult and humbling work of dealing with our own other side.

All too soon the magic wears thin. I loved you in the moonlight, and now I find I have to love you over the dishes. We spent hours dreaming of our perfect future together, but now my feet hurt and you come home at the end of the day grouchy and short-tempered. The better I get to know you, the more we struggle through the hassles of daily life, the more I realize, with a sinking heart, that you, my perfect other self, are not so perfect. The compliments turn into complaints, the hand-holding and candle-light dinners give way to the football game, and instead of a bouquet of flowers you bring me a bag of groceries. And I end up feeling cheated. You aren't supposed to make problems for me, you are supposed to help keep us both in heaven. And you, on your part, aren't entirely enchanted anymore either. Instead of gazing into my eyes, you notice the dust. Instead of taking me out to dine you wave a pile of bills in my face. And we find ourselves in the painful position of wondering whether we still love each other.

This is when types becomes not only an interesting theory, but the lifesaver to our floundering marriage. The projection of falling in love brought us together, and now we are faced with serious typological dirt time. Now I have to look at myself to see what type I am, you have to look at yourself, and we have to look at each other closely so that we will understand why we fell in love in the first place. But the intial instinct is not to settle down to hard work, but to blame the other for all this unhappiness and disillusion. "You aren't who I thought you were." We were as much in love with the image of our own perfection as we were with the actual, living, breathing other person. And the unfortunate result is that I have an unerring instinct of how to upset you, and you know just the right words to send me crying to the bedroom.

But rather than engage in marital warfare it is time to wake up from our dream of perfection and begin to make that dream into a reality. I projected on you because you are my unconscious half, but I can look at you again and learn from you. You already know how to be strong where I am weak, and vice versa. Now I can take the first tentative steps into my unknown half and begin to experiment with new ways of dealing with myself, you, our marriage, and life. And I am a living model of your own weakest parts. Now is the time where we have to join together as we never have before and work toward mutual wholeness. Now is the time for extra tenderness and compassion as we get our courage up to see just how inadequate we are inside ourselves. Now is the time for long talks and gentle embraces as we face each problem and conflict not with hate and recriminations, but by trust and suggestions. If I break out in a sweat when I know we are going to meet new people, you make sure I am not left alone too long because you know my crippled extraversion is suffering in the crowd. If you bring up negative intuitions about impending doom, I carefully waylay your ungrounded fears with soft reassurances. If I want time, introverted time, alone with you, you give up going out with the boys and spend a few quiet hours with me. If you tend to spend without thinking of our dwindling bank account, I take you aside and we look at our typological differences calmly. It seemed like a tragedy when our projections crumbled into dust in front of our eyes, but now, with types to guide us we can begin to love again, but this time with our eyes wide open. Marriage becomes the vessel in which we can both go on our interior journey.

Let me describe a typical situation:

Richard, an introverted thinking type, and Helen, an extraverted feeling type

Eight years of marriage had left them with three children, a half-paid-for house and not much feeling for each other. They had thought themselves a perfect match. Helen admired her husband's orderly and logical nature. She liked the way he could carefully evaluate a situation before he came to a decision. She knew he would be a conscientious provider who would always look out for the economic security of his family. And Richard saw in Helen many of the talents he lacked and wished he had. She was cheerful and outgoing. She knew how to have a good time and she made friends easily. But after they were married they had a much harder time appreciating each other's good qualities. Helen had to admit that Richard was a good provider, but she had never realized how unsociable he was. He was like a wet blanket on any ideas she might have that would make their life more pleasant. He didn't like to go out to parties, and she could barely get him to go out to dinner, still less take a real interest in his appearance. He would wear the same old clothes day in and day out.

Richard had come to the conclusion that Helen never had a real idea in her head. All she had was some wild notions that she never stopped to carefully consider and evaluate. Long ago he had learned not to commit himself to any of her projects, which meant spending the evening with a group of people that he had nothing in common with. And what a knack she had for spending money. She was always buying new clothes or planning how she could redecorate the house, or wanting them to get a new car, even though the old one was perfectly fine - a little beat up, perhaps, but it still ran - or dreaming of some expensive vacation. Frankly, he just didn't trust the way she arrived at making decisions. She could never really explain the reasons behind them. It was always something vague like, "I felt it was the right thing to do."

For Helen, Richard seemed to take all the fun out of life. He always had to weigh and mull over things. He just wouldn't let himself have fun right now. He was always waiting for some day that never

came. By the time he did get around to doing something she had lost all her zest for it.

It would be easy to go on and describe many of
the other common contrasts and oppositions that can
be seen in married couples. There is, for example,
the extraverted sensation husband married to the
introverted intuition wife. She feels stifled because
he is so routine-bound, and he feels disappointed that
she can't seem to handle the many details of taking
care of the home. He is matter-of-factly going about
his life, while she gets emotional because she doesn't
experience the kind of intimacy with him that she
thought marriage would bring. But her image of intimacy is a highly introverted one, and he shows his
affection in deeds rather than words.

The real issue is not in detailing these typical
marital difficulties. It is in facing the question of
whether it is really possible to make marriage the
place in which two people can aid each other in going on the journey of wholeness. I have described the
feeling sessions with which I tried to work through
my memories and dreams and release the energy that
had been imprisoned there. Once I had succeeded in
doing this I was no longer caught up in the past, but
had the strength and freedom to try to tackle the
present. For me that turned out to be the question
of marriage. Now I could see that my normal, everyday awareness embraced most of my first function,
much of my second, but just part of my third and
very little of the fourth. It was my third function
of thinking that was split and polarized. The upper
part of it served the ego, while the lower part
looked downward and was connected with the fourth
function and the unconscious itself. I began to realize
that this third function held the key by which I could
understand my relationship with men and decide
whether I wanted to be married or not. The idea of
marriage had attracted me, but whenever I thought

about it in the concrete I would think of the unhappy
married people I knew, and I did not want to become
trapped like they had. But now I saw there was another reason for my hesitations. Because of the split
in my thinking function I was compelled to see men
in two distinctive ways. Sometimes I saw them
through the upper part of my third function, and then
they appeared idealized, spiritualized and safe. But
other times I saw them through the lower part of
the third function, which was allied to the fourth and
separated from consciousness, and these men appeared
earthy and instinctual with overtones of menace.

In one of my dreams, for instance, an attractive
young priest appeared, representing the idealized,
spiritualized and safe part of my thinking function.
But as I looked at him I realized he was drunk, for
he staggered as he walked toward me. I felt afraid
and threatened. Then he turned into a black man, and
finally into a dwarf. The dream seemed to be saying
that my two images of men were connected. And I
saw that if I truly wanted to get married I would
have to bring these two images together inside myself. If I failed to do this I would project one or the
other on my husband, and I would blame him for the
split that existed inside me. Since I couldn't depend
on my inner thinking that embodied so much of what
Jung called the animus, I was compelled to project
it on men and think of them as unreliable. This kind
of projection was a sure formula for disaster if I
married without resolving it. I talked over the whole
matter with Jim, and we saw that he had a similar
problem but for him the split was in his third function of feeling. Again, one part was allied to consciousness, and expressed itself in the form of an
idealized and spiritualized woman, while the other
part was bound up with the fourth function and was
earthy and instinctual. While I was dreaming of primitive black men, he was dreaming of Polynesian
women. Both Jim and I were introverted intuition

types, but the positions of our feeling and thinking
functions were reversed. If I had qualms about marriage, Jim was firmly against the whole idea. It
seemed to him like a prison in which he would be
subjected to a lifetime of paying attention to physical details, and working at jobs he had no interest
in in order to support a family. He loved to spend
his time going on inner adventures. But now the
inner adventure that had started with the discovery
of Jung's psychological types was gripping us both.
Once we saw splits inside ourselves and the possibility that they could be healed, and in fact were
being healed, not only by our individual work but by
our talks together, a new possibility began to whisper
in the background. What if marriage could actually
become the vessel in which our interior journey could
go on, in which we healed these splits and opened
the way to another stage in the process of individuation?

Jim and I got married, and our marriage actually
did become the way in which we dealt with the
question of the third function. I had to see Jim as
both spiritual and instinctual, and to do it I had to
be in touch with the two parts of my own third
function. He had a similar task. I gave him a model
of what more developed feeling was like, and he gave
me one of more developed thinking. He had to learn
to put up with my evaluations by way of feeling, and
not to insist that thinking was the only way to arrive
at a decision. We were facing each other after each
of us had faced our own past. There was no longer
an idealized man and an instinctual one. The two had
drawn together, both inside me, and outside in my
marriage. This new unity left me more in possession
of myself. I felt a deeper inner strength in using my
mind, in studying new subjects and making decisions
about the kind of life I wanted to lead. The healing
of the thinking function had strengthened me.

The Fourth Function

Although I described our marriage in terms of the third function, the fourth function was never far away. The divisions I discovered in the third function were caused by the conflicting forces of conscious and unconscious, introversion and extraversion, first function and fourth function. The third function contained an inner demand that I deal with the fourth, and the more Jim and I dealt with our third functions the more the challenge of the fourth function loomed up.

What is the fourth function like? When it shows itself negatively it's the child caught in a tantrum, the teenager gripped by an unnamed rebellion, an adult plagued by fears and doubts, or an older person who is touchy and cranky. The fourth function starts an argument, accuses someone of a misdeed or slight, keeps us worrying about the future or causes us to curl up and immerse ourselves in the feelings that we are abused and misunderstood. No matter what our particular type is, the negative part of the fourth function makes us feel impatient, frustrated, confused, irritated, jealous or downright angry. We know when it is activated because we suddenly feel snakes writhing in our stomach, our fists clench, we are about to spit out an unkind remark, our eyes glaze over with fury, or we are swamped with an overwhelming feeling of depression. We know we are not in control, but someone or something has touched our fourth function and set us off.

But all too often we do not see that all this commotion is caused by our own interior chaos coming from the fourth. Instead, we blame a neighbor for insulting us, we harbor deep resentments because the boss does not listen to us, we plot small revenges to get even with someone. In other words, we project those feelings of abuse on someone in our everyday world without ever realizing that the initial trouble is right inside ourselves.

No matter whether we are married or not, living with the fourth function is like living in a marriage of opposites that has already gone bad. Whatever I said before about the wounds of the third function goes triple for the fourth, and whatever energy that the third function contains is small compared to the energy locked up in the fourth. If the past has split our third function, it has turned the fourth into an antagonist who knows, and is, all our weak points. Living with the fourth is like living with someone we can't stand and don't know how to get rid of. We want the fourth to do just what we say, or to get out. We want to pretend that he doesn't live in the same house with us. Let someone else live with him.

The thinking type will leave his feelings to be taken care of by the feeling type. He will let her make the plans for the party, invite everyone, and smooth out any difficulties that might arise, even if he created them in the first place. The intuition type will let the sensation type cook his meals, wash his clothes, make his bed and pick up his socks, all with the rationalization that he is doing important intuitive work and doesn't have time to worry about these silly, mundane, unimportant details of daily life. But these kinds of stategies don't work. The fourth doesn't go away. If we ignore it, it causes all kinds of mischief to draw attention to itself like a neglected child. There's no divorce when it comes to the fourth, and it's a good thing there isn't because the fourth function holds the secret to our wholeness. We have to learn to respect its different way of seeing things as our typological opposite, and find a way in which both of us can give in and create a genuine marriage in which neither side of the personality dominates the other, but rather, one in which both have found a way to work together.

The fourth function has a beautiful and awe-inspiring part of itself as well. Then it's wonderful, energizing, exciting and deeply fulfilling. We have already seen it at work in the magic of falling in love. When I have an experience that comes from the positive fourth it can be numinous or out of the ordinary. I get an almost overpowering feeling of joy. I might be going along in my first and second function way, and suddenly I see the sun streaming through the trees, and it transfixes me with its beauty. It was there all along, of course, but I hadn't been able to really see it through my fourth function of extraverted sensation. Or I pay special attention to a little child, and I am overcome by the beauty of this little creature. He has such a long way to go and so much to learn, but right now, this very minute, he is perfect down to his tiny fingernails.

Just what makes the fourth function different from the others? In the first stages of our development we are taking control of the first function, and with it comes part of the second. Gradually our consciousness expands until it embraces part of the third as well. I have already described how the third function can present its own challenge because sometimes our growth has been arrested there. But the process of individuation when it becomes a question of the fourth function goes beyond the expansion of our consciousness. It is not adding more of the second or third, or fourth function to our first in order to create a super personality in which our ego-consciousness and the first function become more perceptive, effective and dynamic. The conscious personality cannot simply expand and become the center of everything, and when it runs into the fourth function it really discovers how limited its point of view is.

Marriage and the Fourth Function

There is no better way to learn about the fourth function than in marriage. Whether it's in the won-

derful projection of falling in love or in the terrible
feeling that follows a serious fight, the fourth function plays an important role. It's easy to learn about
the positive side of the fourth function when we feel
it in that sense of completion that comes from having someone love us, but it's the negative side of the
fourth function that demands our attention if we are
going to make our marriage work. If you represent
my fourth function and that part of me is split off
and antagonistic, then I am going to end up blaming
you for its negative qualities. And this projection
will inevitably set off your fourth function. It's as
if we are living in a strange double marriage. We are
married to each other and each of us has an interior, invisible marriage partner in the form of the
fourth function. If our marriages within are going
bad, they will destroy our marriage without. And vice
versa. If I can't build a bridge to my own fourth
function, you are going to appear an as ally to the
enemy I have within, or even as the enemy himself.

In the case of Richard and Helen, when Richard
sees her run off and spend money and socialize, he
feels as if his own feelings are somehow out of control. Even if what she is doing is innocent and inconsequential, he feels that she is somehow betraying
him. At the very time when he would need all his
objectivity to understand the legitimacy of her point
of view and allow her to have the freedom she needs
to be herself, he is in the throes of his own fourth
function feeling, which is anything but objective.

Helen, in her turn, is caught by her own fourth
function. When Richard seems withdrawn and unsocial
she immediately feels as if he is locking her in a
prison from which she is never going to escape. But
she can't distinguish which of these feelings come
from Richard himself and which come from her own
stifled thinking function. They both have the knack
for setting each other off and they both build up a
backlog of specific instances in which the other per-

son has hurt them. And the more their own fourth functions are rubbed the wrong way the more they insist that it is really the other person who is at fault. They are missing the real promise of the fourth function because to fulfill it they have to turn within and make contact with this other side. They imagine that their marriage problems are unique. If only they had found the right person all would be well. They don't realize that there are thousands and thousands of other couples who are their same types and fall into almost exactly the same kinds of problems. If they could recognize the typological dimension of their marriage they would have the beginning of objectivity. Then would come the task of typological development, and this development could be powerfully aided by the very fourth function that has caused so much trouble. The fourth function has made their other sides visible, and this is an invaluable beginning, for we can't work on a problem we don't even know exists. The terrible vulnerability we feel to the attacks of our marriage partner can be transformed into a sensitivity in which we can help the other person in the delicate job of gently bringing out their fourth function. It is at this point that the couple has to begin to pay attention to their dreams and memories, they have to go through the painful feeling sessions to heal the splits of the past and they have to reach out to each other during this most difficult of times rather than attack each other at their weakest points.

Living With the Fourth Function

My own marriage had started as a working out of the third function, but since the third is so closely connected with the fourth the day arrived when we had to face the problem of the fourth function. Jim and I both had the same fourth function of extraverted sensation, so we couldn't look to each other for an answer. We shared the same weaknesses and blind spots, but what we could do was face the fourth function together and try to find a solution. What we didn't realize was that the solutions that come from the fourth function have a distinctive stamp. They are not like our first, second and third function solutions because they have to have room to embrace the fourth function and its contrasting way of doing things. Real fourth function solutions allow space for both sides of the personality to express themselves. The first function can't predict what they are going to be like, and this makes them interesting, exciting and even maddening.

As introverted intuition types we loved the freedom of travelling to some new place which would then become the backdrop for new journeys within. And we hated regular jobs which gave us only bits and scraps of time to call our own. But we faced a growing dilemma. We could no longer pretend that we were only introverted intuition types, spiritual flyers, people who imagined they could avoid dealing with the fact they lived in this everyday world. We had come back from nine months of studying and camping in Europe, and decided it was time to have children. This decision gave a new sharpness to questions that we had been postponing. How were we going to earn a living? What kind of career should we follow? Would we ever own our own home? And so forth. Jim found a steady job and our first child was born. But as the months went by we found that the usual solutions to these questions didn't appeal to us. Contemplating a 9-to-5 job with two weeks of vacation a year, a 20 or 30 year mortgage on a house in the suburbs and all the rest made our first function scream. Did we really have to do these things in order to deal with the fourth function? Did we have to accept the common solution? Or could we find our own unique way to meet our fourth function responsibilities?

We have seen how the fourth function spins dreams of magical solutions in the form of falling in love. Well, we began to fantasize about finding our magical solution to the problem of living in this world. What if we could find some beautiful tropical island with trees loaded with fruit and the sea teeming with fish? Then fourth function needs would take care of themselves, leaving us our precious free time for inner journeys. We pored over books about little-known islands in the Caribbean and finally found one that looked ideal. It was called Roatan, located off the coast of Honduras. Eventually, we found ourselves in a rattling DC-3 skimming over turquoise waters coming in for a landing on the island. It was a beautiful green and hilly place with secluded coves of white sand, a reef filled with tropical fish and friendly English-speaking people. But it was also hot, humid and buggy. It had plenty of coconuts, fish and fruit, but most of the other supplies were imported and costly. By 10 a.m. our minds clicked off and we sought out the nearest shade. The fantasy spun by the fourth function was hard against physical reality, and our weakness in the fourth had given us none of the physical and mental tools we would have needed to cope with creating a lifestyle in this faraway place.

We went back home to our apartment and job and pondered again the challenge of the fourth function. It was obviously going to take a great deal of work to find a genuine answer, but still and all, the dream lured us on. So the day came when Jim quit his job, we took our 19-month-old daughter and 3-week-old son, got into our Volkswagen camper and drove off. We had no specific destination in mind - only that it would be nice to live in a natural setting and to follow our inner instinct that said deeper down in ourselves and at the same time somewhere outside existed the possibility of a lifestyle that would allow all the parts of ourselves to develop.

Our first day on the road climaxed with our engine blowing up. Our little home was towed to a distant town and we found ourselves living in a motel and watching our hard-earned savings rapidly disappear. Welcome to the fourth function! I can still remember that weekend vividly. We were awash in the feeling that somehow we had unleashed the uncontrolled forces of the fourth function by daring to enter into its territory. But those days marked a turning point. We sat in our room and pored over a copy of Marie-Louise von Franz's **The Inferior Function,** and it began to dawn on us that the fourth function was not something that ought to happen to us in the form of a magical answer, but it was something we had to work on. It seemed as if the fourth function had two faces, or an upper or lower part. There was the upper fourth function that could be brought into consciousness and used to build a richer life. Then there was the dimension of the fourth function that would never come into the focus of consciousness. The question became, "How much of the fourth function could be made to serve our conscious intentions, and how could we deal with the part of it which could not?"

At one point we decided it would be ideal to start our own business. This would allow us to earn a living wherever we were and free us from the former tyranny of bosses and full-time jobs. Then we went a step further and decided to make it a business in which we used our hands, and thus come into daily contact with the fourth function. We ended up making carved wooden frames backed by mirrors and selling them to stores and at craft shows. But again, theory is one thing and practice is another. I remember the day when we received the shipment of a very powerful router. We carefully set it up, and when we turned it on it filled the room with an enormous roar. That was enough. We turned it off, left, and spent the rest of the day reading books. The next day we went back, turned the machine on again, and went a little further, and gradually we established our small business, and in doing so discovered how much the fourth function could be broadened to a conscious awareness and how much our conscious personalities had to change to accommodate it. It would be nice to think that it is sufficient to spend an hour or two a week in some fourth function activity, and thus appease so it will not disturb us. But the fourth function often demands much more than this. It's one of our basic ways of relating to life, and we simply can't do without whatever the fourth function happens to be. As we worked on our woodworking, our fourth function capacity grew until it could carry an almost normal load. Then we faced another temptation, which was to forget it was still the fourth function and try to make it do too much. Our fourth function wasn't really meant to compete against the first functions of other people. We made our business work and gained a lot psychologically by doing so, but it wasn't a path of heart. It didn't have enough room in it for the more conscious parts of the personality to express themselves. It represented the opposite extreme of the tropical island. We couldn't do without the fourth function and we weren't happy continually living in it. We were testing the limits in each direction in order to find out what was feasible.

But the business did give us a way of solving the problem of earning a living, and as soon as we were comfortable with it our thoughts turned to the next question: "Could we have a home of our own?" We were getting more familiar with the kind of solutions that would please us. We knew that we wanted to build our own home and have no mortgage on it.

This led us to pursue the dream of the tropical island, not in the Caribbean, but in the middle of a forest in the foothills of the Cascade Mountains near Crater Lake in Oregon. There we bought land, built a home and lived in a world where there was no escaping the fourth function. But now, as we struggled to erect a solar greenhouse or learned how to build wood stoves or used cross-country skis, we were coming to grips with the fourth function on our own terms. And the end result was magical enough. We had actually created a setting that demanded that we use all our functions, and at the same time freed us from many outside pressures that would have artificially demanded one kind of adaptation over another.

I have told this story in detail in our book **The Treasures of Simple Living.** But it was a typological story as well. The very buildings we built and skills we mastered were at once a solution to genuine outer questions and a step toward wholeness within. Types had become an instinctive and natural tool in living out our lives.

Books for Further Study

The best source for a further study of psychological types is Jung's **Psychological Types.** In it he not only gives detailed descriptions of each type but even more importantly he makes it clear that a study of types has to do with a study of the whole personality, both conscious and unconscious. Marie-Louise von Franz, one of Jung's closest collaborators, has a small book called **The Inferior Function** in **Jung's Typology** which is based on a series of lectures she gave at the C.G. Jung Institute in Zurich. This, too, is very instructive when trying to get a deeper understanding of the fourth function. The best source of information about Jung's life is **Memories, Dreams, Reflections** which concentrates on his inner experiences and how they gave birth to his psychological theories, and makes fascinating reading.

Man and His Symbols by Jung and his collaborators is an excellent introduction to Jungian psychology, including the process of individuation. **The Living Symbol**, A Case Study in the Process of Individuation by Gerhard Adler devotes 400 pages to one part of one person's inner development. Jung's **The Relationship Between the Ego and the Unconscious** sums up the basic structure underlying the individual case material, while his **A Study of the Process of Individuation,** and **Concerning Mandala Symbolism,** give an idea of how the new center of the personality emerges and what symbolic form it takes. For an incisive analysis of projection see Erich Neumann's **Depth Psychology and the New Ethic.**

For information concerning local and professional groups interested in Jungian psychology, conferences, Jungian libraries, publishers, periodicals and more detailed information about the training programs for Jungian analysts, as well as how to locate one in your area, refer to **A Jungian Psychology Resource Guide.** See back pages for ordering information.

CHAPTER 4
WILLIAM SHELDON'S
BODY AND TEMPERAMENT TYPES

One day, after reading a short description of Sheldon's work, we found a copy of his **Atlas of Men** in the local library. This book contained over a thousand carefully posed fotos of nearly nude men. The children crowded around Jim as he flipped through the pages, and they pointed and giggled. Even though we had learned to see people from the point of view of psychological types, it had never occurred to us to look at their bodies. Sheldon's work was to change that. We began to realize that Sheldon was one of those rare men, like Jung, who had pioneered a new way of tracking who we are. But he wasn't going to make any sense unless we made the effort to open our eyes and learn by practice how to see for ourselves. Let's start by looking at the basics of Sheldon's body and temperament types.

Who was William Sheldon?

William Sheldon (1898-1977) was an American psychologist who devoted his life to observing the variety of human bodies and temperaments. He taught and did research at a number of U.S. universities and is best known for his series of books on the human constitution. He was a keen observer of animals and birds as a child, and he turned this talent to good effect by becoming an avid people-watcher, and out of his observations he gradually elaborated his typology.

The Basic Components of Physique

For his study of the human physique, Dr. Sheldon started with 4,000 photographs of college-age men, which showed front, back and side views. By carefully examining these fotos he discovered that there were three fundamental elements which, when combined together, made up all these physiques or somatotypes. With great effort and ingenuity he worked out ways to measure these three components and to express them numerically so that every human body could be described in terms of three numbers, and that two independent observers could arrive at very similar results in determining a person's body type. These basic elements he named endomorphy, mesomorphy and ectomorphy, for they seemed to derive from the three layers of the human embryo, the endoderm, the mesoderm and the ectoderm.

Endomorphy is centered on the abdomen, and the whole digestive system.

Mesomorphy is focused on the muscles and the circulatory system.

Ectomorphy is related to the brain and the nervous system.

We have all three elements in our bodily make-up, just as we all have digestive, circulatory and nervous systems. No one is simply an endomorph without having at the same time some mesomorphy and ectomorphy, but we have these components in varying degrees. Sheldon evaluated the degree a component was present on a scale ranging from one to seven, with one as the minimum and seven as the maximum.

The Extreme Endomorph - Roundness

The easiest way to get an idea of the variety of human physiques is by looking at the three extremes, even though in actual life the various combinations

 are much more common. According to Sheldon's system a 7-1-1 (seven-one-one) is the most extreme endomorph with minimal mesomorphy and ectomorphy. In this physique the body is round and soft, as if all the mass had been concentrated in the abdominal area. In fact, the large intestine of an extreme endomorph can be two or three times the length of that of an ectomorph. Sheldon likened this abdomen to a powerful boiler room with fine powers of assimilation. The arms and legs of the extreme endomorph are short and tapering, and the hands and feet comparatively small, with the upper arms and thighs being hammed and more developed than the lower arms and legs. The body has smooth contours without projecting bones, and a high waist. There is some development of the breast in the male and a fullness of the buttocks. The skin is soft and smooth like that of an apple, and there is a tendency towards premature baldness beginning at the top of the head and spreading in a polished circle. The hair is fine and the whole head is spherical. The head is large and the face broad and relaxed with the features blending into an over-all impression of roundness. The head is like a pumpkin sitting on a barrel, and the abdomen is like a sphere with the chest attached to it like an inverted funnel.

Sheldon imagined the body of the endomorph as a balloon whose walls were thinner at the abdomen and thicker further away. When the balloon was inflated it was largest at the abdomen and smallest at the farthest extremities. Santa Claus is our society's image of the extreme endomorph.

The Extreme Mesomorph - Muscles

 In the extremely mesomorphic physique, or 1-7-1, there is a squareness and hardness of the body due to large bones and well-defined muscles. The chest area, which Sheldon likened to an engine room, dominates over the abdominal area and tapers to a relatively narrow, low waist. The bones and muscles of the head are prominent as well, with clearly defined cheek bones and a square, heavy jaw. The face is long and broad and the head tends towards a cubical shape. The muscles on either side of the neck create a pyramid-like effect. Both the lower and upper arms and legs are well-developed and the wrists and fingers are heavy and massive. The skin is thick and tends towards coarseness. It takes and holds a tan well and can develop a leathery appearance with heavy wrinkles. Sheldon compared it to the skin of an orange. The hair is basically heavy-textured, and baldness, when it appears, usually starts at the front of the head. The extreme mesomorph is Mr. Universe or Tarzan.

Sheldon's initial work with body and temperament types was based mostly on men, and it is in the description of the extreme mesomorph that we have the most need to develop a corresponding female mesomorphic description. Women on the whole tend to have less mesomorphy than men and more endomorphy. Women who are primarily mesomorphs rarely show the same degree of sharp angularity, prominent bone structure and highly relieved muscles found in their male counterparts. Their contours are smoother, yet the chest area clearly dominates over the abdominal area and both upper and lower arms and legs are well-muscled. The skin tends to be finer than in

the male mesomorph, but shows some of the same
characteristics in terms of tanning and wrinkling.

The Extreme Ectomorph - Linear

 The highly ectomorphic phy-
sique, or 1-1-7, is fragile and deli-
cate with light bones and slight
muscles. The limbs are relatively
long and the shoulders droop. In
contrast to the compactness of the
endomorph and mesomorph, the
ectomorph is extended in space and
linear. The ribs are visible and delicate and the thighs and upper arms weak. The fin-
gers, toes and neck are long. The features of the
face are sharp and fragile, and the shape of the face
as a whole is triangular with the point of the tri-
angle at the chin. The teeth are often crowded in
the lower jaw which is somewhat receding. The skin
is dry and is like the outer skin of an onion. It tends
to burn and peel easily and not retain a tan. The
relatively great bodily area in relation to mass makes
the ectomorph suffer from extreme heat or cold. The
hair is fine and fast-growing and sometimes difficult
to keep in place. Baldness is rare. The extreme
ectomorph in our society is the absent-minded professor or Ichabod Crane.

Body Type Recognition

Once we had grasped these three basic elements
we tried to recognize them in ourselves and our
friends. We, indeed, found some people who were
extreme endomorphs, or mesomorphs or ectomorphs,
with little of the other components, but there were-
n't many of them. Most of the people we knew were
a bewildering variety of combinations, and we prac-

ticed mentally weighing how much of each component they had. Jim, for example, had very little endomorphy. He was one of those infuriating people who could eat and eat and never seem to gain a pound. He had some mesomorphy, but probably not as much as the average man. But he did have a lot of ectomorphy. He was tall and thin with long arms and legs, and a slight stoop to his shoulders. One friend was muscular and lean, while another was muscular and bulky. And so on. And slowly we began to recognize eight basic body types.

We have already met the first three in which one of the components stands out. Sheldon liked to draw a body type diagram on which he plotted the different body types. Here's where he placed the extreme endomorph, mesomorph and ectomorph:

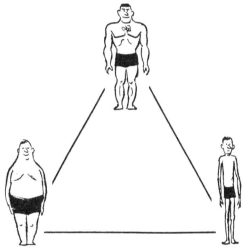

Other people were strong in two elements, and had less of the third. They fell in between the poles of Sheldon's diagram. Four of these combinations captured our attention. There was the hefty muscular person, the muscular thin person, and close to him, the thinner yet still muscular person, and between the ectomorph and the endomorph the person who

was spread out and round without really being muscular.

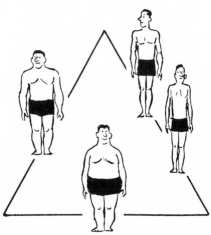

Finally there were the people who had a lot of
each component, and they fell right in the middle
of Sheldon's diagram, and the completed diagram
looked like this:

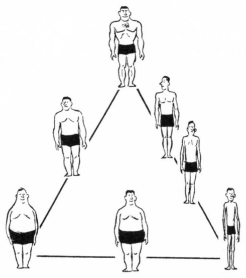

If we take a tour of Sheldon's body type diagram, the endomorph's silhouette looks like a pear. Further up north we meet the endomorphic mesomorph. His abdomen is not quite as massive. His shoulders are bulkier, and this creates a rectangular shape. Much of the softness of the endomorph is gone, replaced by a feeling of solidness. The endomorphic mesomorph is like a bull. Once we hit the extreme mesomorphic pole the bulk of the abdomen has dwindled even further, and there's a strong contrast between the relatively narrow waist and hips and the powerful shoulders and arms. Going down the other side towards the ectomorphic pole we have the ectomorphic mesomorph. He is less heavily built, but still muscular. His neighbor to the south has an equal measure of mesomorphy and ectomorphy, making him thin and muscular. Then comes the more extreme ectomorph, and between him and the endomorph the ectomorphic endomorph, who is perhaps the hardest to recognize. He is spread out and round without being muscular. In the middle are mid-range physiques well endowed with all the basic elements. And somewhere in this panoramic rainbow of physiques is you. Can you find yourself?

Body type recognition is easier than figuring out psychological types because bodies are naturally much more visible. But it is still a skill that has to be acquired by practice. And Sheldon had it in the highest degree. He was a consummate body type tracker. He didn't limit himself to his laboratory photographs, but wandered about beaches and rode the subway in search of interesting and unusual physiques. He could look across a street and tell the difference between a 6-2-3 and a 6-3-2. This level of skill took a lifetime of dedication, but it is possible for us to acquire the basics if we work at it.

One of the unresolved problems of body type recognition is the question of the physiques of women. I have already mentioned that they are more endomorphic and less mesomorphic, but they are also more mid-range. You see more extreme physiques among men than among women, except for the endomorphs. Women are grouped more toward the center of the body type diagram and that makes their somatotypes harder to distinguish from one another. A female ectomorph, for example, often has a lot more endomorphy than a male ectomorph. But still and all, it's possible to find the eight basic body types among women as well as men.

Sheldon's Temperament Types

The classification of body types was not Sheldon's ultimate goal. He wanted to help resolve the age-old question of whether our body type was connected with the way we acted. In short, he wanted to explore the link between body and temperament.

Temperament explores how people eat and sleep, laugh and snore, speak and walk. Temperament is body type in action. Sheldon's procedure in looking for the basic components of temperament was much like the one he used in discovering the body type components. He interviewed in depth several hundred people and tried to find traits which would describe the basic elements of their behavior. He found there were three basic components which he called viscerotonia, somatotonia and cerebrotonia, and eventually named endotonia, mesotonia and ectotonia.

Endotonia is seen in the love of relaxation, comfort, food and people.

Mesotonia is centered on assertiveness and a love of action.

Ectotonia focuses on privacy, restraint and a highly developed self-awareness.

Sheldon devised a way of numerically rating the strength of each area based on a check-list of 60 characteristics (see the end of this chapter) that describe the basic components. The 7-1-1 was the extreme endotonic, the 1-7-1 the extreme mesotonic and the 1-1-7 the extreme ectotonic. He found a strong correspondence between the endomorphic body type and the endotonic temperament, the mesomorphic body type and the mesotonic temperament, and the ectomorphic body type and the ectotonic temperament. Just as in our body type we have all three elements, so, too, with our temperament. A look at the three extremes in temperament will give us some idea of what these components are like.

The Extreme Endotonic - Friendliness

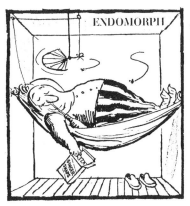

The endotonic shows a splendid ability to eat, digest and socialize. A good deal of his energy is oriented around food, and he enjoys sitting around after a good meal and letting the digestive process proceed without disturbance. Endotonics live far from the upsets and nervous stomachs of the ectotonics. They fall readily to sleep and their sleep is deep and easy; they lie limp and sprawled out and frequently snore.

Endotonics are relaxed and slow-moving. Their breathing comes from the abdomen and is deep and regular. Their speech is unhurried and their limbs often limp. They like sitting in a well-upholstered chair and relaxing. All their reactions are slow, and this is a reflection on a temperament level of a basal metabolism, pulse, breathing rate and temperature which are all often slower and lower than average. The circulation in their hands and feet tends to be poor. Sheldon calls these people biologically introverted organisms. It is as if all the energy is focused on the abdominal area, leaving less free to be expressed in the limbs and face, and giving the impression of a lack of intensity.

Sheldon felt that biological introversion gave rise to psychological extraversion. Since the bodies of the endotonics are so focused on the central digestive system, they need and crave social stimulation in order to feel complete on the social level. Groups of people, rather than fatiguing them, stimulate them to the proper level of social interaction. The assimilative powers that on the physical level were oriented to food, now on the social level draw them to people.

The endotonics love to socialize their eating, and the sharing of meals becomes an event of the highest importance. They treat guests well. They love company and feel more complete with other people around. They like people simply because they are people. They have a strong desire to be liked and approved of, and this often leads them to be very conventional in their choices in order not to run the risk of social disapproval. The endotonics are open and even with their emotions which seem to flow out of them without any inhibitions. Whether they are happy or sad, they want the people around them to know about it, and if others express emotion they react directly and convincingly in sympathy. When an endotonic has been drinking he becomes even more jovial and radiates an expansive love of people. Endotonics are family-oriented and love babies and young children and have highly developed maternal instincts.

In summary, they love assimilation both on the physical and social level. They love to eat and digest, to be part of their family and community, to like and be liked and to rest and relax. They crave food and affection and abhor isolation and disapproval. They express affection and approval readily and need both back in kind.

ENDOMORPHS SEEK COMFORT, KNOW HOW TO RELAX

The Extreme Mesotonic - Action

In endotonia the stomach was the focus of attention, but in mesotonia it is the muscles. The mesotonic is well-endowed with them, or to put it another way, the mesotonic's muscles seem to have a mind of their own. They are always ready for action, and good posture is natural to them. They get up with plenty of energy and seem tireless. They can work for long periods of time and both need and like to exercise. They like to be out doing things. If they are forced into inactivity they become restless and dejected.

The mesotonic tends to eat his food rapidly and somewhat randomly, often neglecting set meal times. He sleeps the least of the three types and sometimes contents himself with six hours. He is an active sleeper who thrashes about. He shows an insensitivity to pain and a tendency to high blood pressure and large blood vessels.

The mesotonic has no hesitation in approaching people and making known his wants and desires. The tendency to think with his muscles and find exhilaration in their use leads him to enjoy taking chances and risks, even when the actual gain is well-known to be minimal. They can become fond of gambling and fast driving and are generally physically fearless. They can be either difficult and argumentative, or slow to anger, but always with the capacity to act out physically and usually with some sort of history of having done so on special occasions.

This physical drive manifests itself on the psychological level in a sense of competition. The mesotonic wants to win and pushes himself forward. He is unhesitant about the all-out pursuit of the goal he seeks. Associated with this trait is a certain psychological callousness. He tends to walk roughshod over the obstacles in his path and the people who stand in the way of his achieving what he wants. On the positive side this is called being practical and free from sentimentality, but on the negative side it is called ruthlessness or obnoxious aggressiveness.

This outward energetic flow makes mesotonics generally noisy. They bustle about doing things and since their inhibitions are low, the attendant noise does not bother them. Their voices carry and sometimes boom out as if speech were another form of exercise. When alcohol reduces their inhibitions, they become more assertive and aggressive. When trouble strikes they revert to their most fundamental form of behavior and seek action of some sort. Mesotonics tend to glorify that period of youthful activities where physical powers reach their peak, or perhaps more accurately the period of youth that best symbolizes a sense of endless vitality and activity. This glorification of youth goes hand-in-hand with the early maturing of the mesotonic organism, both facially and muscularly. They look older than their chronological age. The extraversion of action that is so strong here goes together with a lack of awareness of what is happening on the subjective level. The quickness with which the mesotonic can make decisions is compensated for by a relative unawareness of the other parts of his personality. He tends to be cut off from his dream life. He likes wide-open spaces and freedom from the restraint of clothes.

As we saw in the case of the mesomorphic physique, Sheldon's portrait of the mesotonic is more male than female. The female mesotonic shows the same extraversion of action, but how this action expresses itself has a different quality. There is not the same overt physical combativeness and competitive aggressiveness. The action is more muted and flows in more socially acceptable channels. The mesotonic woman should be compared not with mesotonic men but with other women, and it is in relationship to other women that she shows the distinctive mesotonic traits in a feminine way.

Sheldon felt that estimating the degree of mesotonia was the most difficult part of evaluating a person's temperament. At times people with well-developed mesotonia can give the surface appearance of exceptional calmness and amiability. This is particularly true of the extreme mesomorphs of above-average height who form a kind of mesomorphic royalty. They expect and get special treatment. Sheldon likened them to big cats who go around with their claws retracted, and only when provoked or in the midst of a crisis does their mesotonia show itself clearly.

ECTOMORPHS QUAIL AT PAINS; MESOMORPHS GRIN

The Extreme Ectotonic - Reflection

The outstanding characteristic of the ectotonic is his finely-tuned receptive system. His spread-out body acts like a giant antenna picking up all sorts of inputs. Sheldon calls the ectotonic a biologically extraverted organism, which is compensated for by psychological introversion.

Since the whole organism is sensitive to stimulation, the ectotonic develops a series of characteristic strategies by which he tries to cut down on it. He is like a sonar operator who must constantly be wary of a sudden loud noise breaking in on the delicate sounds he is trying to trace. He liks to cross his legs and curl up as if he is trying to minimize his exposure to the exterior world. He tries to avoid making noise and being subjected to it. He shrinks from crowds and large groups of people and likes small, protected places.

The ectotonic suffers from a quick onset of hunger and a quick satiation of it. He is drawn to a high protein, high calorie diet, with frequent snacking to match his small digestive system. He has a nervous stomach and bowels. He is a quiet sleeper, but a light one, and he is often plagued by insomnia. He tends to sleep on one side with his legs drawn up, and his sleep, though slow in coming, can be hard to shake off. His energy level is low, while his reactions are fast. He suffers from a quasi-chronic fatigue and must protect himself from the temptation to exercise heavily. His blood pressure is usually low and his respiration shallow and rapid with a fast and weak pulse. His temperature is elevated slightly above normal and it rises rapidly at the onset of illness. The ectotonic is resistant to many major diseases, but suffers excessively from insect bites and skin rashes. Unfortunately he can succumb to acute streptococcal infections of the throat which cause swelling and strangulation. His hypersensitivity leads not only to quick physical reactions but to excessively fast social reactions as well. It is difficult for this type to keep pace with slow-moving social chit-chat. He races ahead and trips over his own social feet.

Just as the endotonic loves to eat and the mesotonic loves action, the ectotonic loves privacy. He needs shelter from excessive stimulation and time to sort out the inputs he has received, and connect them up with his own inner subjective experience, which he values highly. Self-awareness is a principle trait of ectotonia. The feelings of the ectotonic are not on display, even though they can be very strong, and so he is sometimes accused of not having any. When they are in a situation of dealing with someone who has authority over them or with someone of the opposite sex whom they are interested in, they often make a poor first impression. They are uncomfortable in coping with social situations where overt expressions of sympathy are called for or where general idle conversation is the norm, for example in parties and dinners where they have no intimate acquaintances.

The ectotonics are hypersensitive to pain because they anticipate it and have a lower pain threshold as well. They do not project their voices like the mesotonics, but focus it to reach only the person they are addressing. They appear younger than their age and often wear an alert, intent expression. They have a late adolescence, consider the latter part of life the best, and are future-oriented. The more extreme ectotonics have a distaste for alcohol and their accentuated consciousness fights alcohol, drugs and anaesthesia and is resistant to hypnosis. They can get in touch readily with their dream life and often nurture a rich fantasy life. When they become troubled they seek privacy and solitute in order to try to work out the difficulty.

ALARM CAUSES VARIED REACTIONS AMONG "MORPHS"

Make an initial estimate of how much of the three components of temperament you have by rating yourself on a simplified Scale of Temperament.

	endotonic	mesotonic	ectotonic
When troubled I seek out	people	action	solitude
I prefer	physical comfort	physical adventure	privacy
The time of my life I favor is	childhood	early adulthood	later years
What would bother me most would be	being cut off from other people	being closed up in small places	being exposed to endless noise
When in a group I like to	mingle	take charge	take off
I prefer to	let things take their course	do things	observe what is going on
The thing I like most is	eating	exercise	time to myself
The qualities that fit me best are	tolerance and love of people	love of power and leadership	a highly developed self-awareness

Seeing Body and Temperament Tracks

Now, once again, comes dirt time. We have to transform our theoretical notions into the practical ability to see body and temperament types as they actually exist in endless and subtle variations and combinations in the people around us. The best way to verify what Sheldon said is to see it for ourselves.

Both Jim and I are more ectomorphic and ectotonic than anything else. Once we began to realize this it explained many things. For the first time we could understand how we could always be feeling tired, and yet be in excellent health, or why we had an intense, almost physical need, for quiet. We could not just tune noise out. It wore us down. One of our best purchases had been earphones for the children's record player. We discovered that we, too, had been engaged in the ectomorph's constant battle against overstimulation. Unremarkable errands in town or normal social visits tired us out much more than anyone realized. We understood, as well, why our minds had clicked off at 10 a.m. in the tropics. Ectomorphs are particularly sensitive to hot and cold weather.

The discovery of our ectomorphy was much like my earlier discovery that I was an introvert. Now I saw it was all right to be an ectomorph. Ectomorphs weren't simply undeveloped mesomorphs, nor were endomorphs overweight ones. Now I could consciously develop strategies to make the most of who and what I was. I needed regular sleep and high protein meals. I had a limited amount of energy to begin with, and I had to spend it carefully.

As I became more aware of my own body and temperament type I could see how I differed from the people around me. Knowing what my gifts and weaknesses were allowed me to appreciate theirs. I saw that my more mesomorphic friends actually re-

velled in a challenge. If some machinery broke down
or some confrontation was brewing, I mentally
cringed, and would have liked nothing better than to
have the problem disappear. But when I looked
closely at their faces, they were actually enjoying
the difficulty and would be disappointed if it went
away. This was their chance to show their stuff.

When I was with my more endomorphic friends
I marvelled at how in tune with their environment
they were. They didn't stint or hold back like I tended to do. Whether it was their emotions or their
money or the story of their life, it flowed out in a
smooth and even tide. They didn't even realize what
a gift this knack of making friends and putting
people at ease really was.

But I also noticed that body and temperament
types had their stereotypes just as psychological
types did. The mesomorph tended to look at the
endomorph as a fat and self-indulgent mesomorph who
had yet to learn the value of discipline. He seemed
to be thinking, "Why don't they get up, work and
sweat off some of that weight instead of finding a
million excuses to avoid the job?" And he looked at
the ectomorph as someone who was sitting on the
sidelines of life. To him the ectomorph was a dream-
er at best, and at worst a loner who could not really
be trusted. The ectomorph was an intellectual who
was driving himself crazy by too much thinking, and
too little doing. He was a stunted and twisted mesomorph.

The ectomorphs, in their turn, were tempted to
see the endomorphs as people who lacked refinement.
They gushed too much; they wallowed in their plea-
sures, and they were constantly touching each other.
They saw the mesomorphs as rude, selfish, pushy and
aggressive people who thought they belonged at the
front of the line. They were given to talking loud
and making crude remarks and riding rough shod over
everyone in their way to get what they wanted, a

bunch of spoilers who destroyed the earth to get their loot, and started fights on any pretext.

The endomorphs viewed the mesomorphs as unfeeling and uncaring savages who lacked normal friendliness and compassion. They were always on the go without time for manners or decent amenities. They were people with no real friends. They saw the ectomorphs as cold fish who never had any feelings and weren't about to get any. They were proud people going around as if they were better than everyone else, and who thought they were too good for normal talk. They were uppity intellectual snobs who were off in some corner up to no good.

Mesomorphic America

One day our young and ectomorphic son showed us, with a wistful expression, a foto of a muscle-building ad in a popular magazine. It featured the usual extreme mesomorph and showed two sketches. The first showed an ectomorph being transformed into a mesomorph, and the second showed an endomorph undergoing the same process. Unfortunately for the dreams of young boys, such transformations simply don't happen. But the ad is a good symbol of America's worship of the mesomorphic ideal. Everywhere we look we see mesomorphs held up as models to emulate. There's the professional athlete, and he's just the pinnacle of a nation-wide program of competitive athletics which gives children the idea that if they only work hard they, too, could become champions. But this athletic version of American democracy and equal opportunity is based on a false premise. While training and the will to win are vital ingredients in athletic competition, we need the proper biological equipment as well. But we are not born with the same amount of mesomorphy and no amount of training is going to equalize these differences. Indescriminate encouragement of athletic competition leads to foreordained results: there are the meso-morphic winners and then people of other body types who are made to feel like losers. Even the majority of mesomorphs are fated to be losers as well. A form of competitiveness that comes natural to the more extreme mesomorphs is enshrined as a supreme value. The end result is body type descrimination.

Off the playing field the same kind of descrimin-ation is evident. Every time we turn on the television we see mesomorphs playing mesomorphic roles that feature aggressiveness and competition. Our ideals of beauty are also highly selective in terms of body type. They run towards primary mesomorphy with a dash of ectomorphy added, and just as in the muscle-building ad or in sports training, the implication is that if only you buy the right clothes, or the right make-up, or go on the right diet, you, too, can be one of these svelte mesomorphic winners. Not only has mesomorphy overshadowed the other two compon-ents of physique, women are pumping iron as if the male mesomorphic model is the goal for everyone.

Even when we turn to the financial pages, we are confronted with more mesomorphic personalities. Here are men and women who have devoted them-selves single-mindedly to making a million, or making it to the top, no matter what the obstacles, and again the implication is, "If we only could get it together, we could make it as well." The plain fact is that the free market is more free for some people than others.

A final mesomorphic model is the politician. In these days when the media packaging of the political personality overshadows content, it is again the mesomorphic image that dominates. It is no accident that athletes become actors and businessmen and turn into politicians. Everywhere we look we see the same message: mesomorphy is best. This is an unhealthy state of affairs, both for the other body types and the mesomorphs as well. It leads to lopsided development. All of us have the basic components of physique and temperament, and all of these components are vital to a balanced and healthy life. Whoever said, "Competition is not everything, it's the only thing" summed up a great deal of our culture. But they had it wrong. That's like saying, "Extraversion is everything and introversion is a disease." There are positive qualities to mesomorphy, and these qualities are part of the reason why mesomorphs are so highly visible in public life. They are active and energetic extraverts who know how to get the job done. But the down side is there, as well. They can be over-aggressive, callous and unfeeling, bossy and intolerant. Even someone who is an extreme mesomorph has an endomorphic and ectomorphic side that is crying out for development.

Body and Temperament Type Development

What does body and temperament type development mean? It means we have to recognize just who we are in terms of what kind of body we have, and what kind of physically conditioned temperament, and meet their particular needs. For example, what is our proper weight? A glance at the height-weight table, even when it is divided into small, medium and large frames is not always adequate. Our proper weight depends not only on height and age, but on our particular body type. Sheldon in his **Atlas of Men,** for example, provides the normal height-weight patterns for 88 distinct body types. It's much the same when it is a question of the kinds and quantities of food we should eat. Body type goes beneath the skin. It's the outward picture of different metabolisms. There is no one ideal diet. It has to be crafted to the kind of body we have. The same is true for exercise. It's pointless to set up one program for everyone to participate in. We don't have the same hearts or lungs or muscles. The same vigorous exercise that would energize the mesomorph and make him ready to tackle the day would exhaust the ectomorph, and leave the endomorph far back in the dust. This doesn't mean that the ectomorphs and endomorphs are excused from exercise, but they have to find the exercise that fits their own particular needs. The endomorph may take up swimming, and the ectomorph a non-percussive type of exercise like yoga. Body type development is made more difficult by something that Sheldon called dysplasia. There's no guarantee that we possess the same kind of body type in each part of our body. A boy with a normal masculine physique can have arms like a girl so he can't throw or fight, or a girl can have hips that are over-sized, or an athlete might be a top-flight competitor except for the fact that his legs are too weak.

Although body type tracking starts with recognizing the kind of body we have, it soon becomes a way of making the most of it. And this strategy goes beyond the attitude that society fosters. It's not enough to develop the gift we have. We can't relegate the mesomorph to the playing field and the ectomorph to the library. Each of us has less developed parts of ourselves that need attention. The ectomorph or endomorph can become a well-conditioned ectomorph or endomorph. The endomorphic lady can find her own version of slimness, even if this means weighing more than her friends. But in all these cases the underlying body structure will not go away. It will not become miraculously transformed, and we can avoid years of frustration trying to do what we are not endowed to do when there are many gifts that each of us have that remained undeveloped.

At the level of temperament we can call the three basic components amiability, action and reflection. And we need all three. I am more reflective than anything else, but when it comes to doing chores around the place being reflective will not get me very far. I have to reach down in myself and draw out my own mesomorphy. I need extraversion of action if I want to get the woodshed filled. And being reflective doesn't work when friends drop by for a visit. They didn't come to watch me read a book. This time I draw out my amiability or extraversion of affect to make our visit enjoyable.

It would be possible to describe the typical conflicts in marriage from the point of view of different body and temperament types like we did in terms of psychological types. Here are two people who have different needs and speeds. He wants to go jogging and she wants to read a book. He thrashes about or snores when he sleeps. She's cold and he's hot, and they fight over opening the window. Such mundane details are part of every marriage and can become the focal points of contention. How much easier it would be if we could see the other person's body and temperament type objectively and stop trying to make them over into our own image.

It took us months of work before we had grasped the basics of body and temperament types and could track them with anything near the facility we had recognizing psychological types. Then we were tracking two very different kinds of tracks made by the same elusive human. Or were we?

Books for Further Study

The best source of detailed information on body types is to be found in Sheldon's **Varieties of Human Physique** and the **Atlas of Men.** The **Varieties of Human Physique** contains detailed descriptions not only of the three extreme body types or somatotypes, but many others as well.

The **Atlas of Men,** which contains photographs of over 1,000 different male physiques, is a fine tool for gaining an overview of the different somatotypes. In it Sheldon describes one of his methods for estimating body type, which is based on height and weight, and a visual inspection of the photographs.

The best description of temperaments is Sheldon's **Varieties of Temperament** which contains six full-length case studies, as well as a more detailed presentation of the matieral we have used in this chapter.

CHAPTER 5

TWO TRACKS IN ONE

Body and temperament types had grown from a footnote to our interest in psychological types into a full-fledged way of seeing that complemented what Jung had done. The next step was both inevitable and exciting. We knew that Jim and I were both introverted intuition types and ectomorphs. Was this an accident? A friend who was an extraverted thinking type we now saw was a mesomorph. We had never averted to either his physique, or single-mindedness, or booming voice or all the other mesotonic traits he possessed. Another friend was predominantly endomorphic, and we already knew that she was an extraverted sensation type. Were body and temperament types randomly distributed among the different psychological types, or were they organically connected? Intrigued, we began to systematically examine the body types of all the people whose psychological types we already knew. This helped confirm our initial insights. There seemed to be a definite connection between the endomorph and the extraverted sensation type, the mesomorph and the extraverted thinking type, and the ectomorph and the introverted intuition type.

The best way for you to determine whether such connections actually exist is to go tracking yourself and look at the body, temperament and psychological type of someone you know well and see what you find. There is really no substitute for this kind of personal verification. Once we had some idea of what we were looking for, then, and only then, did it become possible to reread Sheldon and discover nuances we had missed before. Here's a summary of Sheldon's remarks on the endotonic, mesotonic and ectotonic that point to their respective psychological types.

The Psychological Type of the Endotonic

The numbers in parentheses refer to traits in Sheldon's **Scale of Temperament** and the page number to his **Varieties of Temperament.**

The endotonic is an extravert. He loves to have people around, a trait Sheldon called sociophilia (8). He is dependent on them for affection and approval (10). The endotonic does not hold back his emotions; whatever is there flows readily and smoothly out (17) and can be easily understood. He wants to be around people when he is troubled (19). He is well-oriented to the social world around him and knows what the general opinion of the community is about many individuals in it (11).

The endotonic has sensation as his first function. He is oriented to the world around him through his sense impressions. "Endotonics can always be trusted to maintain a close grip on immediate practical reality." (p. 249-50). "Endotonia means realism. Endotonic ecstasy lies in the achievement of a 'real' surrounding made up of nice things that taste good, smell good, look good, sound good, feel good." (p. 253). He loves to eat (4) and to be physically comfortable (2), and he likes people simply because they are with him without making judgments about them (9). They are facts which he accepts (13).

The endotonic has intuition as his fourth function. He tends to lack foresight and a sense of progress. He is not a reformer (16). He views the ectotonic as a "dark and suspicious person, a miser at best and a sinister influence at worse" (p. 37) which is a good description of the negative intuition of the extraverted sensation type.

The Psychological Type of the Male Mesotonic

The mesotonic is an extravert, with relatively little grasp of his inner self (17). His is an extraversion of action. He loves physical adventure (2) and is full of energy to be doing things (3). He is physically courageous for combat (8) and has an unrestrained voice (13). He dislikes being enclosed in small places (11).

The first function of the mesotonic is thinking. The mesotonic knows what he wants and he has a "singularly impersonal objectivity in seeking what is wanted" (p. 55). He is effective in carrying out decisions without inhibitions. He is stable, predictable and hardheaded (p. 58). He gets things done without always stopping and considering the physical and social costs (p. 59). "The even regulation of habitual overt behavior in mesotonics is striking, but it is perhaps relatively unimportant in comparison with the same habitual ordering of mental activities" (p. 265). This habitual ordering of the mental activities is a result of the predominance of the thinking function.

The least developed function of the mesotonic is feeling. The negative side of the efficiency in getting things done is callousness towards people and things that get in their way (11). As Sheldon puts it, they have a "singular insensitivity, especially to the less obvious or subtler needs or desires of other personalities in the environment" (p. 57). On occasion the unconscious feeling suddenly reveals itself in the form of sudden conversion with religious overtones (p. 65) which represents the introverted feeling side of the personality.

The Psychological Type of the Ectotonic

The ectotonic is an introvert. "The thing to be saved and protected at all costs is the continuity and the integrity of the inner awareness. Such a person disassociates the outer objective reality but remains in the closest touch with his own inward subjective reality."(p. 88). The ectotonic loves privacy (4), tends to avoid much socializing (8) and is restrained both in voice (9) and in the expression of emotions (6).

The most developed function of the ectotonic is intuition. He has a great deal of curiosity and moves from one new interest to another. "He seems to be able to change his mind abruptly and suddenly adapt all his feelings and attitudes to the new orientation." (p. 82) He is oriented to the future (20) and wants to understand the riddles of life (p. 93). "One of the most striking characteristics of persons showing the C-17 trait (introversion) predominantly is their acuity and preciseness of intuition. Intuition is of the first order in these people, for it is based on a thorough familiarity with the remote consciousness from which it springs." (p. 89).

The least developed function is sensation. He cannot seem to accept physical realities matter-of-factly. He has difficulty in forming routines and habits (10) and difficulty in learning things by rote. He either ignores things or reads too much into them. "Ectotonics desire but little, but they seem to become inordinately attached to what they have both in the sense of material goods and in the sense of personal loyalties." (p. 37). Physical objects become alive to them. "He becomes affectionately attached to things, reads human qualities and feelings into them and often focuses deep affection upon things that are not human." (p. 255). He can have an especially difficult time dealing with sexuality. "The ectotonic is always in danger of flying too far from the earth and suffering an Icarian fall" (p. 250).

Sheldon's body type diagram now looks like this:

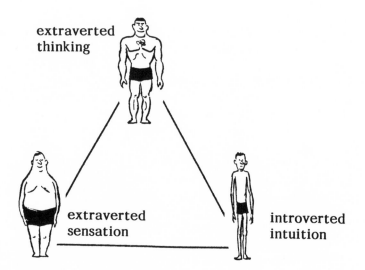

extraverted
thinking

extraverted
sensation

introverted
intuition

But what were the physiques of the other psychological types? Finding out was a harder task. Reading
Jung or Sheldon couldn't provide an answer. It had
to come from someone who actually left certain
body/temperament and psychological tracks. We were
already familiar with the ectomorph who was an
introverted intuition type. But what about a man we
knew who we were sure was an introverted thinking
intuition type? He was more mesomorphic and less
ectomorphic than the ectomorphs who were introverted intuition types. He was built trimly like a mara-
thon runner. He was what Sheldon would call a
2-4-4, which meant that he was equally mesomorphic
and ectomorphic with little endomorphy. Once we had
him as a good first example we took a careful look
at some other introverted thinking intuition types,
and found that they had similar builds.

Then there was a friend who was our favorite
example of a zany and exciting extraverted intuition
type. He was more muscular than the introverted
thinking type, but he still had a good deal of ectomorphy. I think Sheldon would have rated him around
a 2-5-4.

The endomorphic mesomorphs who are one of the most popular American somatotypes turned out to be either extraverted sensation types if they were a bit more endomorphic, or extraverted thinking sensation types if they were somewhat more mesomorphic. The body type diagram now looked like this:

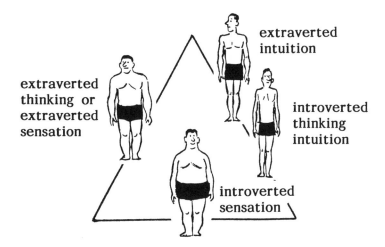

This left the introverted sensation type, the introverted thinking sensation type and the question of women. Eventually we placed the introverted sensation type between the endomorph and the ectomorph, and the introverted thinking sensation type became a good example of how type theory has to flow from type practice. It would have been convenient to put the introverted thinking sensation type with the introverted thinking intuition type, but we found an introverted thinking sensation type whose body did not seem to fit this pattern. It was more chunky and less ectomorphic. Then we found several other introverted thinking sensation types who had similar physiques. They still remain a puzzle. Here, however, is how our body type diagram finally looks:

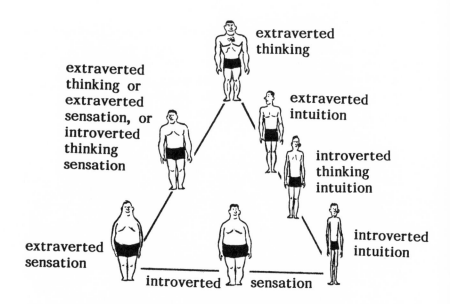

extraverted
thinking

extraverted
thinking or
extraverted
sensation, or
introverted
thinking
sensation

extraverted
intuition

introverted
thinking
intuition

extraverted
sensation

introverted
intuition

introverted   sensation

Women follow the same pattern as men but they are more difficult to somatotype, for they are more endomorphic and more closely grouped together. This means there are less women who are extreme mesomorphs and more women who are well-endowed with endomorphy. Women, for example, who are introverted intuition types will have in general more endomorphy than their male introverted intuition counterparts. Women are more naturally midrange and more grouped in the center of the body type diagram. So a relatively small difference in somatotype can be the sign of a large difference in psychological type. Instead of the mesomorph being an extraverted thinking type she is usually an extraverted feeling type, and the introverted thinking intuition types and introverted thinking sensation types become introverted feeling intuition types and introverted feeling sensation types. In short, to convert the above diagram from men to women replace thinking with feeling.

All this sounds a bit complicated, but if we study these diagrams there is a certain interior logic in them. Let's imagine that each of the three corners is like a magnet, and each of these magnetic poles has its strongest influence on the area that is closest to it, while its power of attraction weakens with distance. The ectomorphic pole is associated with introversion and intuition, the mesomorphic pole with extraversion, thinking and feeling, and the endomorphic pole with extraversion and sensation. If we stand on the ectomorphic pole and look towards the mesomorphic one, we see that intuition and introversion grow less strong as we move towards the mesomorphic pole of extraversion, thinking and feeling. The introverted intuition type becomes the introverted thinking or feeling intuition type, then the extraverted intuition type and finally the extraverted thinking or feeling type.

These diagrams should not be taken as finished products. A great deal more experience is necessary to determine exactly where the boundaries between the types are. Detailed body and temperament descriptions like those of Sheldon for the three extreme somatotypes remain to be written for the other psychological types. What follows are tentative notes on the body and temperament type of each psychological type.

The Introverted Intuition Type, the Extraverted Thinking Type and the Extraverted Sensation Type

We have already seen Sheldon's description of the body types and temperaments that correspond with the extraverted sensation type, the extraverted thinking type and the introverted intuition type. The thing to note is that while Sheldon was describing the extremes of each somatotype, the territory of each psychological type covers a wide area made up of many somatotypes and temperaments. We should not expect the introverted intuition type to always resemble a bean pole or the extraverted sensation type to look like Santa Claus.

The introverted intuition type covers a wide range of physiques from the walking stick to the slim muscularity of the mesomorphic ectomorph to the midrange balanced body types. In the same way the temperament varies and no doubt the psychological type itself within the territory of the introverted intuition type.

The extraverted sensation type ranges from the roundness of the polar extreme to the burliness of the endomorphic mesomorph who might actually have more mesomorphy than endomorphy and he, too, shares in the midrange balanced somatotypes, who at first glance seem almost the same as the midrange physiques that belong to other psychological types.

The extraverted thinking type ranges from the extreme polar mesomorphs to the extraverted thinking sensation type who is heavy-set and chunky under the influence of the endomorphic pole and the extraverted thinking intuition type who is leaner but still heavily muscled, who is closer to the ectomorphic pole.

The Introverted Sensation Type

The Body Type

The physique of the introverted sensation type is that of an endomorph-ectomorph, sometimes with little mesomorphy, but ranging up to the midrange body type. We should not think of the roundness of the endomorph as an opposite to ectomorphy. The introverted sensation type has a roundness which is extended and spread out in space by ectomorphy. In this way he can be distinguished from the predominant endomorphy of the more extreme extraverted sensation type who is more spherical at the endomorphic pole and more muscular furtner north on the somatotype chart.

The Temperament Type

The introverted sensation type shows a special type of ectotonic behavior due to his introverted sensation. He has a love of privacy and is restrained in voice and in the expression of his emotions. He does not have the easy extraversion of affect of his neighbor the extraverted sensation type. His emotions, while strong, are held in and shyly bestowed. He does not exhibit the quick friendliness, tolerance and indiscriminate amiability found in the extraverted sensation type. He can set a good table but does not make the same social sacrament out of eating.

The ectotonia of the introverted sensation type takes on a different character because sensation replaces intuition. The introverted sensation type is more orderly and meticulous with details and observant of routines. Their houses are often particularly neat and clean in marked contrast with the introverted intuition type who sins by omission and inadvertence, and the extraverted sensation type who fails by lack of organization. They show none of the quick curiosity and reaction and movement from one topic to another characteristic of the ectotonic introverted intuition type.

He shows little of the love of risk, chance and competition that is found in the mesotonic. He is by nature conservative and conserving. He tends to keep what he has and keep it well. When he accumulates money it is more from careful use than daring entrepreneurial acts.

The Extraverted Intuition Type

The Body Type

The physique of the extraverted intuition type is

that of the ectomorphic mesomorph. His ectomorphy makes his muscles stand out in clean, sharp relief so that the degree of mesomorphy could tend to be overestimated at first glance. The extraverted intuition type often gives the impression of lean muscularity and speed. The 2-5-4 somatotype which Sheldon likens to an ocelot or cheetah falls in this range. Petersen in his **Atlas of Children** remarks about one of his 2-5-4 boys, "He loves freedom above all and does not want to be tied down to anything whatsoever. Seemingly his most profound need is to be independent."

The Temperament Type

The extraverted intuition type shares the extraversion of action of the more mesotonic extraverted thinking type. There is a love of physical adventure and an enjoyment in being out and doing things. He is outgoing and physically courageous but without the same aggressiveness and love of domination that marks the more extreme mesotonic. Neither does he share the mesotonic's knack of rubbing people's feelings the wrong way. He is quick in movement and accident-prone, and his tolerance for pain is mixed with a certain amount of concern for his health. Instead of being youth-oriented he is future-oriented.

He shares the ectotonic's intuition, but not his introversion. He looks to the future outside, changes activities quickly and resists habit and routine. He chafes under authority and loves freedom and independence.

The extraverted intuition type forms a strong contrast with the endotonia of the extraverted sensation type. He is fast to react, slow to relax and unwilling to take time out to eat. While being warm and friendly among the people he knows well, he shows little of the tolerance and indiscriminate amiability of the extraverted sensation type.

The Extraverted Feeling Type

The Body Type

The range of the extraverted feeling type covers much of the territory of the extraverted thinking type but with fewer people at the polar extremes and more in the midrange since most extraverted feeling types appear to be women. The extraverted feeling type territory might also extend further south than the extraverted thinking type territory but have the same basic separation into the extraverted feeling sensation type and the extraverted feeling intuition type.

The Temperament Type

The extraverted feeling types show the mesotonic extraversion of action and are generally energetic and well-liked. But this is female mesotonia with feeling in the first place instead of thinking, and so the male mesotonic qualities like love of physical adventure, risk and chance and combative aggressiveness are all toned down. The extraverted feeling types can be athletic, lively and assertive without being combative. The extraverted feeling type's muscles, while not as pronounced as the male mesotonic's, make nicer curves and they have an effect physically in the high energy level and temperamentally in the ability of this type to control and dominate a situation with a combination of physical presence and focused feeling. People tend to want to do what they want them to do. Like the male mesotonic, the female looks with nostalgia on youth as the time of physical perfection. They tend to mature earlier and feel older earlier, and be concerned about their beauty fading.

The Introverted Thinking and Introverted Feeling Types

The Body Type

It appears that these types cover two distinct territories; one next to the introverted intuition type, which has the introverted thinking intuition type and the introverted feeling intuition type, and another on the other side which contains the introverted thinking sensation type and the introverted feeling sensation type. Since this is the only instance where a type territory is split up there is a chance that we are mistaking a portly 4-4-4 introverted thinking sensation type for a more endomorphic and/or mesomorphic physique which would place the introverted thinking sensation type and the introverted feeling sensation type on the other side. It is striking, however, that all the types with sensation in the first or second place fall on the left side of the diagram and the introverted thinking sensation type and the introverted feeling sensation type fit into this pattern, so we will describe these types as living in two separate territories.

The physiques of the introverted thinking intuition type and the introverted feeling intuition type often, at first glance, look like the mesomorphic introverted intuition types. Some of these two types are long and thin, but with a closer examination they show a greater degree of wiry mesomorphy than the introverted intuition types. The introverted thinking sensation type and the introverted feeling sensation type appear to cover part of the same territory as the more mesomorphic extraverted sensation type.

The Temperament Type

The introverted thinking intuition type and the introverted feeling intuition type share many of the traits of the ectotonic introverted intuition type with whom they share their introversion and to a lesser degree their intuition, such as love of privacy, emotional restraint, as well as a reluctance to socialize. In a lesser degree they share the quick reactions of the more extreme ectotonics and what Sheldon calls mental over-intensity or hyperattentionality. The introverted thinking intuition type, because of the placement of the thinking function, has what could be called an introverted or mental mesotonia in contrast to the more physically active mesotonia of the extraverted thinking type. He does not boom out vocally or try to dominate a social situation, but he has an inner hardheadedness and mental drive, and it can produce through the inferior feeling function a disregard and callousness or obliviousness to the feelings of others that mirrors in its own way the inferior feeling of the mesotonic.

The introverted feeling intuition type differs from the introverted thinking intuition type much like the extraverted thinking type differs from the extraverted feeling type. The traits due to introversion remain in place, like love of privacy, etc., but the character of the mesotonia changes to a more feminine one without the same ruthlessness that comes from feeling in the fourth place. The introverted feeling intuition type can sometimes appear somewhat lifeless because the feelings are not immediately visible.

The introverted thinking sensation type and the introverted feeling sensation type can be mistaken at first glance for more or less amiable extraverted sensation types. Despite appearances they possess little of the sociophilia and smooth extraversion of feeling that is the hallmark of the endotonic. They share with the rest of the ectotonics a certain distinctive self-conscious movement of the eyes. It is almost as if they are introverts in extraverted bodies.

The introverted thinking sensation type can be a businessman with a difference. He has the mental equipment to pay attention to practical detail combined with the introvert's instinct for preservation. Add to this a love of competition and dominating and a dash of ruthlessness that comes from the mesotonia and it can be a formidable combination for material success.

The introverted feeling sensation type will again differ in characteristic fashion with the ectotonic love of privacy, sociophobia, vocal restraint and secretness of feeling but without the sense of competition and domination found in the introverted thinking sensation type.

Complete Type Tracking

It has been essential to cover the basics of type at all three levels. And perhaps you have some idea of what your own complete type is. But be patient with yourself. It will take real work to convert all the principles, examples and descriptions of the preceding chapters into your own ability to see types. It's not possible to grasp everything at once. When I meet someone for the first time I wish I could say that I can readily figure out their type on all three levels, but it doesn't work that way. Sometimes I might be sure that the person is a mesomorph, or their fourth function is feeling, or that they are an introvert. And I have to be satisfied with these relatively modest starting points and let my understanding grow naturally by my contact with them. So don't be discouraged if you are sure of only a small portion of your own type. Your ability will grow with practice. I have included more notes on the eight types from the point of view of body, temperament and psychological development in the appendix, but it is up to you to breathe life into this theoretical knowledge by trying to use types day by day.

PART II
TALKING ABOUT TYPES

We have all had the experience of reading a book or listening to a lecture and wanting to say, "Now wait just a minute," and ask a question that would help clarify the subject for us. Therefore, I have tried to pose and answer some of the questions that come to mind while reading **Part I.**

C.G. Jung's Psychological Types

A friend of mine went to a Jungian analyst and they never discussed types. You seem to be implying that psychological types is equivalent to the process of individuation. Is it?

Yes. It is certainly possible to deal with the process of individuation without mentioning psychological types, not that I am saying that this is an ideal state of affairs, but it is not possible to deal with the full scope of psychological types without considering them from the point of view of individuation. In fact, I feel that types represent the most visible and tangible way of approaching the question of individuation. They are a wonderful antidote for anyone who thinks that Jung's psychology is other worldly or mystical. Types help us see that the quest for individuation should be part of the ordinary affairs of our daily lives.

Some books I have read have left me with the impression that Jung abandoned psychological types after his book came out. Is this true?

No. Jung wrote his first essay on psychological types in 1913, then he put a great deal of effort into refining his initial ideas on introversion and extraversion in the years up until the publication of **Psychological Types** in 1921. Types was the doorway through which he approached the process of individuation. Once he went through the door he didn't have the same need or inclination to speak about them, but he did continue to indicate that he had in no way abandoned them. This can be seen in the essays on types he wrote after 1921, in his letters, and interviews. Another reason why he didn't speak much about types was because he felt that they were not properly understood in relationship to individuation, and so there was no point in making ever more refined comments when the basics were not being grasped.

How did Jung decide that there were eight types?

He first described introversion and extraversion, and then felt that that was inadequate, and after a great deal of discussion and pondering he came to the conclusion that there were four kinds of introverts and four kinds of extraverts. But this wasn't a theoretical conclusion. This is what he finally saw in his patients, friends, etc. So there weren't eight types because he thought there should be eight types. There were eight types because that's what he found.

Are we born a certain type?

It certainly appears that way. Jung was struck by the fact that very young children have highly distinctive personalities even when they grow up in the same home. While he didn't minimize the powerful impact of parents on shaping their children's personalities, he felt that psychological types were innate. And I think a lot of parents would agree with him. The same probably holds true for body and temperament types. There have even been studies of infants where the researchers divided the children up into suckers, kickers and watchers, which would be roughly equivalent to Sheldon's endomorphs, mesomorphs and ectomorphs.

Then why do people talk about their types changing?

The fact that we are born a certain type is not opposed to type development. It means we are inclined to certain developmental pathways rather than others, and if we stray too far from our own pathway, if, for example, we are an introvert and someone tries to bring us up as an extravert, then we are storing up trouble for the future. But within our own pathway there is ample room for our unique development. The reason why people talk about their types changing is because they are experiencing the dynamic process of type development. Sometimes it is a question of discovering their own type after a long time of accepting society's or other people's definitions of who they are. At other times, it is a matter of the introvert making contact with his more extraverted side, or the feeling type with her thinking, and so forth. And so they experience how they differ from what they were before. But I think that if we take a larger view of the matter, it's not so much a question of becoming a different type but rather progressing in the process of individuation in which we discover that we somehow have to embrace all the different kinds of types within ourselves. In other words, instead of saying, "I was one type and became another," if we look deeper we would see that we were one type and now we have broadened that type by experiencing deeper levels of that same type. An introvert, for example, by going through this developmental experience, will be more extraverted as he becomes acquainted with and uses his third and fourth functions.

I know someone whose type I can't figure out even though I have tried and tried. Why is it so

difficult?

Type recognition, in the concrete, is enormously complex. There is no guarantee that our first impressions of another person convey something about their dominant attitude or principle function. It may be that we meet someone, and it's their inferior function that creates our initial impression of them. In other words, we can experience many different aspects of the other person's type, and it can be difficult to decide what is coming from the developed, more conscious side of the personality and what is coming from the unconscious. The whole problem is made even more complicated by the fact that we are all in various stages of development, and so we are continually changing our type appearance. In addition, when we are engaged in creative activities we are reaching down into the other side of our personality and so this, too, can mislead someone about our type. Neurosis, as well, if we understand it as an uncontrolled breaking forth of material out of the unconscious, makes type recognition more difficult.

All this is just one side of the question. We are looking at this enormously intricate totality, which is the other person, but we are looking at them from our own typologically conditioned perspective. We are looking at the other person through the colored glasses of our own type. Sometimes, we will be really keen in discerning a certain aspect of their personality, but at others we will be blind to what is right before our eyes. All these reasons make type recognition a skill we have to learn, a skill which is intimately connected with our own development, and not something we can master simply by reading a book.

I can't decide what type I am. Would it help to take a professional type test?

It might. But don't expect the test to produce

magical results. Let's suppose the best of all possible outcomes; you take a type test and it actually does indicate what your type is. The creators of these tests make it clear that this doesn't always happen for a variety of reasons, but let's suppose that in your case it does. This can only be one step in the process of the discovery of your own type. Just because we know the words doesn't mean we understand their implications. If the test tells me I am an extraverted intuition type, those words remain ineffective until I have a concrete grasp of what extraversion and intuition are. In short, the test is an aid to help us in the process of type discovery, and we can't let it take the place of our own attempts to see typologically.

If the test gives us a wrong answer there is no way to tell whether it is right or wrong unless we have learned how to make our own typological judgments. Right or wrong, tests don't excuse us from putting in dirt time.

Does anyone know how many introverts and extraverts there are in the United States?

I don't think so. My own guess, and it's a rough one, drawing on some of the results that have been generated by type tests, and some of our own work, would put the figures at around 40% introversion and 60% extraversion. This makes the U.S. an extraverted country, but it acts a lot more extraverted than the figures suggest. That's because the extraverts are running it. Other countries are more introverted, but world-wide most countries are trying to imitate a Western extraverted model.

You seem to be implying that most men are thinking types and most women are feeling types. Is this true?

This is a difficult issue. As soon as we start talking about gender roles it is hard to peer through the thick fog created by our stereotypes about men and women. But, yes, I do think that most men have thinking as the first or second function, and most women have feeling as the first or second function. This is a position that finds some support in Jung's remarks in Chapter 10 of his **Psychological Types,** and is based on our own experience. When we have met men who have feeling as one of the first two functions and women who have thinking as one of the first two functions, I have found them to be interesting and intriguing personalities. In the women, for example, their thinking has no tinge of what Jung calls the animus possessed woman, a sort of ambivalence in which thinking is swayed by emotions. It has a solidness and clarity that is very appealing. Feeling in the first or second place in a man is equally distinctive. I think these people have particular problems adjusting because society doesn't understand them. There's a difference between these people and a much larger group of men and women who have developed their thinking and feeling functions.

How much difference is there between two people who have the same type except that their second functions are different?
The second function makes an important practical difference in our types. Both Jim and I are introverted intuition types, but I have feeling as my second function and he has thinking. Sometimes when he is going on and on about different intuitions, I first enjoy the process because of my own intuition, but then I get tired because my intuition is feeling-toned and so if he is describing all the places we could live, for example, it is theory to him, but I feel myself living first in one place and then another, and end up exhausted. Or if Jim starts discussing something in a theoretical way I like to turn the discussion to concrete examples.

Can you give me an example of what it is like to work on the third function?

My own third function is extraverted thinking, while Jim's is extraverted feeling, and there are situations in which we are both involved in a business matter, and instead of Jim bringing his thinking function to bear and me my feeling function, we are in our third function mode. This means he's relating to the person we are dealing with, while I am left with the task of doing the negotiating and nailing down the business decisions. This, incidentally, illustrates why type recognition is so difficult because it looks like he is the feeling type and I am the thinking type.

One time when we were designing frames for our mirrors, Jim did some with graceful curves, coming, no doubt, from his feeling function, and I created one that was like a sunburst with pointed rays. What a mistake! Almost all the ladies who bought this piece exhibited characteristics of the animus possessed woman. Most of our sales were straightforward, but for this mirror the women wanted to buy it but were compelled to make all sorts of negative comments. They would haggle about the shape, the construction and the price in a way that was quite uncharacteristic of the rest of our customers. It got so bad that I would expect trouble when a woman began to show interest in it, and I wasn't disappointed. It just seemed to bring out the ambivalence that can come from the third function of thinking.

You can experience the negative impact of the third function in many ways. Some of my favorite examples are among women who work as bank tellers, clerks or secretaries. They know the rule book inside out, or think they do, and they have definite opinions about how things should run. How many times have you gone to the bank, or you make a business call because you need information, or you are trying to get through to the boss and the secretary says, "I'm sorry, sir, he can't be reached," "I'm sorry, sir, it can't be done." "I'm sorry, sir, we don't handle that," when you know all along the boss is right there smoking his pipe, or the organization can, and did, in fact, handle that matter, or can give you that information. It is not so much what she says, but the way she says it, and her tone gets you in the guts. She has a certain tone of definiteness, of immovability, of absolute sureness of what she is saying even though she is really incorrect. And she won't let you talk to anyone else, either! She believes she is Reasonableness, personified, and you, with your irregular request, are the unreasonable one. It is as if she really doesn't want to make the effort to think on her own, and you are forcing her to do it.

Does individuation mean that eventually we will no longer have an inferior function?
I wish it did! There is a great deal of progress we can make in dealing with the fourth function. It can be a lot more functional than we ever imagined. It doesn't have to be, and cannot be, relegated to some kind of esoteric hobby. But at the same time the fourth function remains the fourth. If it could become as developed as the first function it would no longer be related to the unconscious, or we would have turned the unconscious completely into consciousness, which is impossible. The fourth function is like an object bobbing on the surface of the ocean. Sometimes we see it well on the peak of a wave, but at other times it disappears. We can't bring it into perfect focus. It's as if we are thinking about something else when we should be concentrating on the fourth function activity. It just slips away from us.

Why does our fourth function get upset so easily?
After Houdini's mother died, whom he was very

close to, he would have liked very much to believe in communications from the dead. But he was a trained magician, so he would go to all sorts of seances and try to discover how the mediums were doing their tricks. I suppose he was hoping to find one who was legitimate. Before one session he tied something around his leg so his leg became tender and swollen. Then during the seance he could feel the medium move her leg in order to create the special effects. Well, the fourth function is much like Houdini's leg. It's tender and sensitive, even hyper-sensitive, and it doesn't take much to set it off. We don't have to wait for someone of the opposite type to do it, though they may have a special knack. Anybody's fourth function can set off our own. It's like a contagion. Have one person in the family succumb to the fourth function, and if they don't pull themselves out of it, sooner or later they can set everyone else off, as well. I might be feeling good because everything is going well, and then I get tired or overstimulated, or my hormones change at the end of the month, and my fourth function is ready to explode. Or things may be going fine and I feel I am finally getting everything together when, for no reason I can put my finger on, I start losing things, forgetting things, making stupid mistakes, and so forth. I think overall we make progress, but it's not smooth progress. It can come in fits and starts, and we can suffer reversals and dig holes for our-selves which we have to climb out of.

Does the midlife crisis have anything to do with type development and the fourth function?
Yes, I think it does. The fourth function with its particular kinds of difficulties can often apear at what Jung called our second half of life, which is usually around our 35th to our 37th year. For many of us our energy up until this point has been directed outwardly to things like education, career, marriage

and family, getting our own home, material security, etc. Let's suppose we have been modestly successful in accomplishing these goals which represent our status of being an adult in this society. Then one day, much to our surprise, we find that we don't have the energy we used to for these things. We are puzzled by our lack of enthusiasm and wonder if we are somehow losing our grip. This can lead us to intensify our use of our one-sided consciousness. Our sense of dissatisfaction can be projected outward in the search for a new mate or new career, but often these attempts to reinforce who we are make us feel even emptier. What is happening? It just may be that we have entered a new stage of development at the heart of which is the fourth function. More of the same is not going to work. What we need to do is to become attentive to the demands of the other side of our personality.

There is no reason to believe that all types go through the same kind of midlife development. What I have just described would seem to fit extraverts more than introverts. You meet people who have finally arrived at their time to introvert. But what about the introverts? It may be that they finally arrive at their time to extravert, or to make it a little more nuanced, there can be various rhythms and patterns of introversion and extraversion that weave their way through the days, weeks and years of our lives.

Do you think most marriages are marriages of opposites?
I don't know. There are certainly enough of marriages of complete opposites to make them a useful example of the kinds of projections that go on in falling in and out of love. And I would think that every marriage, even if the two people are exactly the same type, which I don't think happens very often, would still have a large measure of

projection and working out to do because we are dealing with two distinct people who have their own stage of development, and, indeed, their own unique voyage into the unconscious to make. The dynamics that I described in terms of marriage will fit, in their own way, the relationship between parents and children, and other close relationships. What goes on between the analyst and the analysand in terms of transference and countertransference can be seen as an example of similar processes that fill many of our important relationships.

What about types and school? My son is bored and restless. Could part of the problem be his type?

That's something to look into. I have enough difficulties dealing with the distinct types of my children when it comes to education, even though I know what their types are and I am teaching them at home. Therefore, I am sympathetic with the school teacher who is faced with thirty children of all different types at different educational levels and she has to teach a set curriculum, test them and grade them. On top of that, school as an institution doesn't have, as yet, any real awareness of type differences. Like so many institutions, it is concerned with imposing one way of doing things on everyone. The end result is a form of schoolroom discrimination. Instead of it being the introverts and ectomorphs being descriminated against, I think at times it is the other way around. Many ectotonic introverts do well in academic situations, but pity the poor extraverts who are loaded with energy and are supposed to sit still and be quiet for most of the day. No wonder they are constantly squirming around. And think of the endomorphic extraverted sensation types who are socially and visually oriented. These people are highly reactive. They like to interact with people, and they need that kind of interaction in order to get themselves up to speed, as it were. Is it any wonder that they tune out? I think it would be a lot different if school activities could be much more concrete for them, more hands-on and tangible. And imagine the intuition type who is already three jumps ahead of everybody, but has to wait while everyone slowly and laboriously does everything step by step. Sheer torture.

To get back to marriage for a moment, would you advise people of opposite types not to marry?
Who can say? Or perhaps more to the point, who is going to listen, anyway? We are attracted to the power and sense of completion that comes with these kinds of projections in marriage. They tell a story of how Kibbutz children from different families who have grown up together communally look elsewhere for marriage partners. One girl said, "How can I marry a boy who grew up sitting on the next potty?" We want projection, for we equate it with romance and love, but let's look at it this way. If one of our children wanted to marry someone from a very different culture, I would certainly be concerned that they were aware of these differences before the marriage took place. Well, this kind of common sense should be extended to types, as well. The more opposite the person is, the more time and energy we should spend before the marriage in trying to truly understand their viewpoint. Hopefully, this would short-circuit some of the projections which are so nice in the beginning, but soon become hard to handle. We feel smugly superior in the fact that our marriages are based on romance instead of parental arrangements, but we haven't learned how to come to grips with the projections this implies.

Sheldon's Body and Temperament Types

I am interested in psychological types. Is it important for me to learn about body and temperament

types as well?
You can't do everything at once. In fact, it might be better if you are starting out to choose either psychological types or body and temperament types, and get a handle on one of them lest everything get confused.

Which one should I do first?
I could make a case for either side, but I think I favor doing psychological types first. The reason is that Sheldon left the therapeutic side of his psychology undeveloped. He does make some interesting comments about development, but most of his energy went into description. Jung's psychological types, on the other hand, are part of his whole psychology, and that means they have a readily grasped therapeutic or developmental dimension. But still and all, follow your own inclinations and insights. The two complement each other beautifully, and they form a much more complete typology than one alone. It's like body and soul. The basics of body types are easier because they are visible, but more difficult because they lend themselves less well to type development. Psychological types are just the reverse.

I have heard the names ectomorph, mesomorph and endomorph, but I have never really heard anyone talk extensively about Sheldon's work before. Why not?
Sheldon championed what he called constitutional psychology, which was a biologically oriented psychology, at a time when such an approach was not popular. This led to his work being involved in a lot of controversy, and the controversy formed a smoke screen that tended to prevent people actually trying to become conversant with it. They did not become body and temperament type trackers, and without that skill his psychology didn't find the applications it could have.

I have gotten heavier as I have gotten older. Has my body type been changing?

No. Simple weight changes as we get older or if we go on a diet don't change our somatotype, for the somatotype is based not just on surface appearance but tries to take into account the underlying bodily structure. Our weight history is just one element that goes into determining our body type. Sheldon has height-weight graphs for many somatotypes in his **Atlas of Men** in which we can see how most types gain weight as they grow older, and then lose weight late in their lives.

I have a general idea of what my body type is, but is there some way I can determine it more exactly?

There are a variety of methods which depend on photography and/or taking measurements of different parts of the body. Perhaps the easiest method, one that doesn't demand the use of special equipment, is the one that Sheldon proposes in his **Atlas of Men.** He provides a chart by which we can determine our height over the cube root of our weight, and then use this number, together with our age, to find what somatotypes are in our own area. Then we can compare our physique with the photographs in the **Atlas** and arrive at a relatively good estimation of our somatotype number.

I noticed that while you had Santa Claus and Tarzan as examples of the endomorph and mesomorph, is there a better example of an ectomorph than Ichabod Crane?

Your question points to the fact that ectomorphs are not public figures to the degree that other types are. If I were going to look for examples of prominent ectomorphs I would look among scientists and scholars, especially mathematicians and theoretical physicists.

One ectomorph who has received a great deal of nation-wide attention is Bernhard Goetz, the man who shot four teenagers in a New York subway. A **Time** magazine article described him "with his hunched narrow shoulders, his chin tucked resolutely into his chest, and his slinky, slouched walk, Bernhard Hugo Goetz looks rather like a human question mark." And, "The original, eerily accurate police drawing of Goetz showed the face of the "before" figure in comic-book ads for body-building devices, the pale visage of the scrawny, bespectacled fellow at the beach who gets sand kicked in his face by a burly bully." Then they went on and described his personality as "gentle but demonstratively violent. Personable, but introverted. Idealistic, but cynical. He desires privacy, but has courted publicity. He is humble, but strangely messianic." And when he was interviewed, Goetz kept saying all he wanted was privacy.

Goetz is an ectomorph and ectotonic, and probably an introverted thinking intuition type or introverted intuition thinking type, though that is just a guess. And I find it interesting that even though he became a public figure with partisans on both sides, he remained an enigma as illustrated by **Time** magazine, treating him like a paradox with his desire at once for privacy and publicity, humble and messianic, etc. He just didn't have the kind of personality that the American public could unambiguously embrace, even if we leave aside the reason for his fame. Abstracting from his own personal problems, part of the incomprehension that surrounded him was precisely because of his type. There is a highly introverted conscious personality and the less developed extraverted side with feeling and sensation.

Can a midlife crisis be related to body and temperament as well as psychological type?

I think so. Sheldon noted that ectomorphs are

often late maturers in contrast to mesomorphs, who mature early. Ectomorphs often marry late, make career choices later on in life, and mature mentally well into middle age. They give the appearance of being less adapted to outer events, but this lack of adaptation can be seen in a positive light as well. The ectomorph, in order to deal with an outer event, has to deal with the inner impact and implications of that event, and therefore his outer adaptation tends to be a more complete adaptation. I would imagine that both ectomorph and mesomorph cope with the second half of life in different ways. The ectomorph could well have been dealing with the question of the other side of his personality during much of his adult life, but slowly and in connection with his problems of outer adaptation, while the mesomorph arrives at the second half of life with a firmer grasp of the outer world, but with fewer clues about what his inner adaptation should be.

If body types don't change, why is it that I seem to be seeing a lot more muscular physiques in both men and women?

There are three factors we should look at. The first is a positive one in which more people are taking an interest in physical fitness. They are making the most of the mesomorphy they have, and it shows. The second aspect is less positive. Jung once commented that he thought that America was "as extraverted as hell," and Sheldon, in the early 1940s, thought that the United States was in the midst of a mesomorphic revolution that was overturning the ectotonic values of an earlier age. What would he say today?! There is certainly nothing wrong with being mesomorphic. We all are in one degree or another. But when we accentuate this aspect of our personality to the detriment of the others we are headed for trouble. We don't want to be just muscular and competitive.

This brings us to the third factor, which is artificially induced mesomorphy, or mesomorphy at any price. I am talking about the wide-spread use of anabolic steroids. We have so exalted professional athletics in terms of recognition and material reward that it has become a prime symbol of our overaccentuation of the mesomorphic part of our personalities. Therefore, it is hardly surprising that steroids are so widely used, despite the health hazards involved. But since body type is so closely connected with temperament, the use of steroids produces personality changes as well. People become more competitive and aggressive and more intensely single-minded, all qualities that may have some payoff momentarily on the playing field, but can have a negative impact on the quality of life as a whole. We are entering a new era where the potential for the manipulation of body, temperament and psychological type will be much greater than ever before. If steroids represent an artificial mesomorphy and LSD and mescaline an artificial intuition and introversion, then the wave of the future is going to include human growth hormones, which will be used as a form of artificial ectomorphy or height, and many other products produced by genetic engineering. The only real remedy is a thorough understanding of what our complete personality is like, that the goal is individuation and not overaccentuation of one part of the personality at the expense of the rest.

Can you give an example of some well-known figure whose body, temperament and psychological type agree with the connections you have made?

It is always tempting to illustrate typology with public figures, but not only do some types predominate more than others among public figures, but public personalities have highly developed personas, or public images, so they don't necessarily make the best examples. But let me try anyway. Let's take someone whose somatotype is unmistakable. I think everyone would agree that Arnold Schwarzenegger is an extreme mesomorph. Sheldon describes men who are high in mesomorphy, for example, the 2-7-1, as "lions and Bengal tigers. Strongest, heaviest, most compact of the modern great cats...The traditional royalty of the animal world." And Arnold describes in his autobiography the impact he wanted to make in his bodybuilding contests. He "wanted to move like a cat, going gracefully from one pose to the next, making a lyrical sweep and then hitting it with power: Boom! Just like a cat when it jumps - making this beautiful, silent jump - then landing with a lot of noise and force. A cat kills, a big cat. And that's what I wanted to do."

And he shows many of the characteristics of the mesotonic. Mesotonics, for example, don't like small, enclosed places. For Arnold it wasn't just a room or a closet. He felt that all of Austria wasn't big enough for him! He describes himself in his early days, "I already felt I was better than anyone else. I felt as if I were a Superman or something. That was my attitude: macho. I was strong and I walked the streets feeling and acting tough. If someone made the slightest remark or gave me trouble I would hit them over the head. I was aggressive and rude. I'd go into a beer hall where we ate dinner after training and start a fight for no reason at all." And he summed up his philosophy of life, "The meaning of life is not simply to exist, to survive, but to move ahead, to go up, to achieve, to conquer."

And it is possible to interpret some of his remarks in terms of his psychological types as well, which I imagine to be extraverted thinking. He wanted, for example, to make his body look like that of the famous muscle-builder Reg Park. "The model was there in my mind." And he single-mindedly tried to implement his plan of becoming the best-built man in the world, and let nothing get in his way. "I knew the secret (of success): Concentrate while you're training. Do not allow other thoughts to enter your mind." If thinking was his most developed function, feeling was least developed. While he was involved with many women on a physical level, he guarded his feelings. "I couldn't be bothered with girls as companions. My mind was totally locked into working out, and I was annoyed if anything took me away from it. Without making a conscious decision to do so, I closed a door on that aspect of growing up, that vulnerability, and became very protective of my emotions. I didn't allow myself to get involved - period. I grew accustomed to hearing certain questions: "What's wrong with you, Arnold? Don't you feel anything? Don't you have any emotions?""

I noticed that this is Volume I. What is in Volume II?

Volume II is about the formal study of types. It asks questions like, "How did psychological types develop out of Jung's life and works?" "What happened to psychological types after 1921?" "What new developments have there been in the field in recent years?" It also presents a detailed study of Sheldon, who was one of America's best, yet least-known, psychologists, and it looks at some of the criticisms that surrounded his work. It goes on to explore the question of a biochemical typology, and looks into the interesting issues of type and mental disease, type and heart disease, and type and genetics.

I am puzzled about your diagram (p. 120) in which you show the endomorphic-mesomorph as being either an extraverted thinking type or an extraverted sensation type, or an introverted thinking sensation type. Can people of this physique have three different psychological types?

As far as the extraverted thinking types and the extraverted sensation types, it means this is where the two type territories meet. The more muscular endomorphic-mesomorphs are extraverted thinking types, and the more endomorphic people are extraverted sensation types.

In the case of the extraverted thinking sensation types and extraverted feeling sensation types, I have seen men and women who seem too chunky and muscular and too lacking in ectomorphy to be placed with the introverted thinking intuition types. I don't know where to put them. Whether the different type territories overlap is something that could only be determined by using sophisticated methods of somatotyping on people whose types are well known. I am inclined to think that they don't overlap.

By likening types to tracking are you saying it is more an art than a science?

I am trying to emphasize that it is a skill that needs to be learned by practice. Sheldon compared somatotyping to stock judging at county fairs and to wine tasting. Both Jung's and Sheldon's typologies emerged out of their personal experience and were developed in systematic ways. But this scientific elaboration rests on concrete experience and is meant to serve concrete goals, like how to help someone go on the journey of individuation. If we make typology into a science which forgets to look at individuals, we soon become enamored with the theory of typology and forget it is about understanding you and me and helping us grow. Psychological types, for example, is rooted in Jung's entire psychology but in itself it is a practical science. Therefore, typology is something we learn by doing. Whatever we study has to be transformed into our own personal insight by contact with people of different types. Happily the raw material is all around us!

What would be a good way to learn this practical science?

When our family meets someone new we frequently discuss our type impressions afterwards. Our son might say, "Well, he is certainly an intuition type." or our daughter might comment, "He was no extravert!" And so a discussion will ensue which often leads to a fairly unanimous judgment. I think that an effective way of learning about types would be to create a slightly more formal version of this family assessment. Any small group could present cases, as it were, by discussing their own types and seeing if everyone can agree. This can't be done cold. We need a certain amount of knowledge about the person, but this knowledge is not particularly hard to come by. What's hard is its interpretation.

Jim and I have done typological interviews where we give a person with no knowledge of types a capsule summary of the basic elements. For example, we explain the difference between introversion and extraversion for a couple of minutes, and then have that person decide what predominates in them. Then we go on to thinking vs. feeling, and sensation vs. intuition, and finally which of the functions is strongest. This is often surprisingly effective.

A small group of people interested in learning more about types could stage their own typological interview. How a person enters a room, his hesitations or lack of them in speaking up and making small decisions, his personal history, how he responds to a type interview, etc., all can be good signs of what his type is, and the group could learn to interpret them.

Sheldon, in fact, created a temperamental interview of this sort and a roughly organized psychological type interview along the same lines, which could include a psychological type test and a discussion of its results, would be a valuable tool for type training. It is easy to see how its use could be extended to any number of job and school situations when basic typological knowledge would be invaluable.

APPENDIX

NOTES ON TYPE DEVELOPMENT

This appendix, which looks at body, temperament and psychological types from the point of view of development, will draw the different levels of type together and serve as a summary for **Part I** at the price of some repetition.

There is no prescription that will spell out how to develop your type. You are a certain type but in a particular and individual way. Your own path of development will be unique inasmuch as it draws on your personal history. No one will have your dreams or fantasies in exactly the same way. No one else will possess the foreign language of your inner world that you must learn to translate. So from this point of view there can be no set rules of behavior or dictionary of dream symbols that will relieve you of the task of exploring your inner world.

But if you go exploring without any compass or maps, you have a good chance of getting lost and in trouble. When Jung set out to travel in the unconscious, he had to fashion his compass as he went along. We, at least, can take advantage of his work and make our own journey safer. We have some tentative charts and landmarks to go by, but we still have to get up and go.

The following remarks on the development of the types, therefore, are not prescriptions to be handed out to each type, like advice dispensed from a fortune-telling machine. They are just hints about situations you might encounter in your own journey into the inner psyche.

The Development of the Extraverted Sensation Type

The Body Type

We have seen how the body type of the extraverted sensation type varies from the pole of predominant endomorphy to that of the endomorphic mesomorphy. It is crucial to keep this in mind when reading the descriptions here which fit the more extreme endomorph and have to be more and more modified as the body type varies.

The extraverted sensation type is the champion at eating, sleeping and relaxing. They love food, and have an almost irresistible tendency to gain weight, for they extract the maximum benefit from what they eat. Our present American diet of highly refined foods with the fiber removed and calories added is precisely the wrong diet for them. In an attempt to feel full they consume more calories than they use.

The weight problem of the extraverted sensation type is aggravated by his low metabolism and his inclination to relaxation. He does not burn up energy in muscular tension or in exercise as readily as other types. This means more weight, which in turn leads to less exercise and still more weight. For the extraverted sensation type who is high in endomorphy but low in mesomorphy, getting enough exercise is a difficult task. Exercise in this context does not have to mean jogging or calisthenics, but simply direct physical action like walking to the corner store and working in the garden, etc. Swimming is not only a well-rounded form of exercise, but endomorphs do well at it because of their buoyancy.

The extraverted sensation type who is high in mesomorphy often combines a high level of direct physical action, exercise and excessive weight. The weight is more spread out and less noticeable in appearance, but the combination still tends to overload him. This somatotype territory is prone to coronary heart disease.

The extraverted sensation type likes to sleep and does well at it. He is therefore inclined to oversleep which, of course, does little to help the weight problem. The primary endomorphy of the extraverted sensation type tends to buffer them from the full development of their ectomorphic component. This component is a need for quiet and a sense of listening. The endomorph is biologically introverted with his energies focused on his physical well-being. This is in sharp contrast with the biological extraversion of the ectomorph whose body is exposed to all sorts of stimuli like a giant antenna. The endomorph is compact and has proportionally less of this receptive ability. Therefore, he needs to make a special effort to have a definite quiet time to help in his listening to these more distant messages, which often carry important information about his inner self.

The Temperament Type

The extraverted sensation type displays a wonderful extraversion of affect by which he makes other people feel at ease because of is own amiability, complacency and tolerance. He tends to be openhearted and open-handed, and have a strong sense of family. But these positive qualities do not exist in a vacuum. They are linked with the less developed aspects of the same temperament.

Unless extraverted sensation types are high in mesomorphy, they tend to lack a certain drive and discipline to get jobs done. Their habit of amiable acceptance makes it hard for them to be consistent disciplinarians. Their open-handedness with their money leads to budgetary problems. They can profit from making a budget or a list of chores for their children or themselves, to make what is to be done more tangible and objective, and hopefully more achievable, but the roots of the problem lie deeper than this.

The very sociability of the extraverted sensation type is linked with his difficulty in making use of quiet time to reflect about himself. His biological introversion is compensated by a psychological extraversion. He likes, needs and wants to have people around. But this extraversion makes it more difficult for him to deal with his introverted side, which has to do with reflection about the goals of his own personal life. The extraverted sensation type who takes an hour to go for a walk by himself, or to sit in a quiet place, not to meet everyone or notice everything, but simply to be alone and have a gentle inward focus, may find that this practice allows him to deal with his own personal decision-making better and to consider where he has come from and where he is going. This kind of active listening is not to be confused with a passive feeling of inertia that is related to the sense of depression sometimes found in this type.

The extraverted sensation type on the body and temperament level possesses virtues, but these virtues are connected with vices, or to put it another way, each positive quality is linked with an undeveloped or even negative quality, and real development is a process of forming a new center which takes both sides into account. Extraverted sensation types can eat well and do so, but this good quality often leads to overeating which has an effect on their physical and social well-being. Instead of eating being brought to the temperamental level in the form of a social sacrament of eating, where they are at the table with their friends and family in good fellowship, they incur social disapproval and are called fat people. This leads to guilt and secret eating. The wonderful sense of relaxation and tolerance of other people that they possess as a natural attribute can lead to their being the victims of intolerance where they are called shiftless and lazy. Their heart-warming flow of feeling towards other people can have its negative side as well, where they find themselves being fended off for being excessively sentimental and affectionate.

All the other types have problems, each in his own way, and each type cannot reach a full measure of growth and happiness simply by depending upon their most conscious and developed gifts, without the development of the weaker and less conscious part of his personality.

The Psychological Type

The possibilities of development are even more ample at the level of psychological type, and here the balancing of the various components takes a deeper meaning and leads to a new center of personality.

The extraversion of affect we saw at the level of temperament becomes transformed into extraverted sensation. Extraversion of affect is not to be confused with Jung's extraverted feeling. The feeling of the extraverted sensation type follows in the path of the sensation function. His feeling is at the service of the extraverted sensation energy, and so it does not have the focused quality of extraverted feeling as a first function. Sheldon could say that they like people simply because they are people. The extraverted sensation type's enjoyment of people does not depend on careful scrutiny of them.

The use of the auxiliary functions allows the extraverted sensation type to discriminate, evaluate and follow through on their objects of interest. In this way, the second and third functions of either thinking or feeling are equivalent on this level to what mesotonia is on the level of temperament. It is the feeling and the thinking functions, to the degree they are aiding the first function, that let him acquire the drive, discipline and active pursuit of the outer goal that will allow him not only to sense what is around him but to act on this perception for his own good. The higher the mesotonic component in the extraverted sensation type, the easier this energetic action is to begin with. An extraverted sensation thinking type or an extraverted sensation feeling type finds some difficulty in learning to use the third function, for it is another way of evaluating things, and they are used to the old way. The extraverted sensation feeling type, for example, who has good social follow-through, has to work at developing a logical follow-through that is useful in other situations.

Somewhere in the functions is the door that leads to the introverted side of the personality. Often it is in the third in many adults. They have conscious use of the first, some of the second, and a bit of the third. When this is not true, the process of development takes a different course, for the second and third functions need to be more integrated before the problem of the other side can be tackled.

Since the fourth function of the personality is the least known, we cannot turn directly to it and try to draw it into consciousness. The lower part of the third, which would be either introverted feeling or introverted thinking, forms the bridge to the introverted intuition. It is here that we need the various methods that we have discussed, namely dreams, fantasies and experiences of high feeling intensity. Any one of these three methods can provide access to what is happening in the world below. Once we gain some insight we must not simply look at it but try to figure out what practical steps we can take to integrate it into our lives.

The Extraverted Thinking Type

The Body Type

On the whole extraverted thinking types are energetic and active. No one has to be after them to get exercise. Their high energy output lessens the chance of them becoming overweight. However, when they dwell in the territory right next to the extraverted sensation type boundary they can put on pounds and their drive which can be even more intense than the extraverted sensation type can lead to health difficulties.

The more mesomorphic the extraverted thinking type is, the less he shares the endomorph's love of food and his relaxed style of eating and digesting. The extraverted thinking type often eats infrequently and voraciously, and is not inclined to sit and relax or spend much time sleeping. He gets by on the least sleep of all the types. The extraverted thinking type has to learn how to let his endomorphic component come out. He should take time for regular, well-prepared meals, preferably with other people, and spend some time eating and socializing without trying to do something else as well. He can benefit from just sitting and letting himself relax. This relaxation can be a way of approaching the question of time for himself and listening to his inner demands. The relentless drive of the extraverted thinking type to accomplish his plans conflicts with the conditions he needs in order to see what his plans are doing to him on a personal level. An all-consuming plan can bring him to a state of ruining his health and alienating the people around him. On the basic level of ectomorphy he has to stop and take time to listen to his own inner demands and those of the people he loves.

The Temperament Type

The extraverted thinking type excels in direct decisive action in the face of obstacles without which many jobs in this world would be left undone. But this positive aspect is connected with a negative one.

Decisive action becomes ruthlessness; direct execution becomes callousness to the feelings of others, and a love of challenge becomes a love of domination.

Mesotonia must leave room for endotonia. The extraverted thinking type needs to spend time with his family and friends without constantly looking at his watch or sitting on the edge of his seat. He can profit by trying to like people because they are people without considering how they fit into his plans.

Mesotonia must also come to terms with ectotonia. It is only with a modicum of privacy and freedom from incessant pressures that the extraverted thinking type can listen to the messages coming from his own body and psyche. He needs time to dream and focus on the world within. This inner world holds the answer to psychic growth and health.

The Psychological Type

We have already described the basic structure of this type with his first function of thinking and how the second and third serve to strengthen it. The first phase of development is this strengthening and expanding of ego consciousness. This often happens more or less naturally as we grow up and try to use our best talents to make our way in the world. Unfortunately, the very kind of specialization and differentiation of functions that allow us to play a part in society leads us to one-sidedness in our personal development. The extraverted thinking type must develop the auxiliary functions, but this alone will not lead to complete development.

The second phase of development deals with the question of the fourth function and the relationship between the ego and the unconscious. This kind of development is not fostered in the same way by the world we live in. It is not as immediately evident that we are undeveloped in this sense, for we can carry out a normal role in society without it, but it does make a great deal of difference in terms of our personal health and happiness and the state of psychic health of the world in general.

The extraverted thinking type often uses the lower part of the third function to make contact with the fourth. He has to be careful that he does not try to simply rope it into consciousness. For example, the intuition of the extraverted thinking sensation type is partially allied to the conscious personality, and as such is a source of valuable new ideas. When he approaches and contacts a deeper part of the intuitive function he is liable to expect it to produce more new ideas that will be of use in his overall conscious plan. The real value, however, of the introverted part of the intuitive third function lies in what it can say about the ultimate meaning of life rather than the help it can give in starting a new business. It is only by overcoming great inward resistances that the extraverted thinking sensation type can accept as a reality this kind of message. Introverted intuition which contemplates the goals and purposes of the inner life must be accepted more for itself, and the extraverted thinking sensation type must ask himself, "What purpose does my inner life have?" "What is to become of all that I have?" "What is the purpose of being?" When these questions become real questions, they lead to introverted feeling by which he faces the question, "What is it that these kinds of values have to say to me?" "What does the love I have for my wife and family really mean to me?" In this way the inner world begins to open up, and if it is accepted and taken seriously, it modifies the conscious personality and its behavior.

The Introverted Intuition Type

The Body Type

There is a considerable range in the body type of the introverted intuition type, as we have seen, and each of these somatotypes would have a different developmental path, but with some common characteristics. The ectomorph has a finely-tuned nervous system, and a highly developed self-awareness. With this radar he is constantly picking up not ordinary sense impressions but signals from beyond his immediate environment. He is a biologically extraverted organism, and his acute perception of these signals comes at the price of tending to be abstracted from concrete sense details.

The more unbuffered by endomorphy he is, the more he must protect himself from overstimulation. His nervous system can become overloaded in situations that other types take for granted, e.g., by crowds, shopping trips, or noise. They have the highest need for quiet of all the types.

The ectomorph with little endomorphy tends to have a short length of intestines, a small stomach, a high basal metabolism rate and a considerable energy output from muscular tension and a highly charged nervous system. Therefore, he needs a high protein, high calorie, easily digestible diet with frequent feedings of smaller portions. Breakfast is important so as not to draw down his energy supply. The introverted intuition type who is an endomorphic ectomorph, on the other hand, will tend to be overweight like the extraverted sensation type.

The ectomorph is often a light sleeper and a poor one; he can use a full eight hours, and sometimes a catnap during the day is helpful in order to give his overworked awareness a rest. The same purpose can be served by some light distracting recreation. Even with a lot of sleep ectomorphs can suffer from a chronic sense of fatigue and be depressed from no other cause than low energy. He must protect his energy supply both from overstimulation and overexercise. In contrast to the mesomorph, instead of a real workout invigorating him, it can leave him moping around for the rest of the day. Some exercise, in a non-jarring form, like cycling, yoga or walking, can be very beneficial in bringing out the mesomorphic side. The ectomorph, when he is extreme, needs to carry what weight he can as a form of padding, and make judicious use of social contact and exercise as a way to bring him out of himself without causing exhaustion. In cases of exhaustion caused by overstimulation, the introverted intuition type often responds to solitude and quiet.

The Temperament Type

The introverted intuition type is the most ectotonic of the psychological types. They put first the development and the continuity of their inner awareness. They are constantly receiving inputs from within and without, from both far and near via their intuition. If they are to receive their faint, distant signals, they must shield themselves from excessively strong stimulation in the foreground. They spend their energy linking up their new feelings and thoughts, intuitions and sensations to the past with the desire to be able to grasp past, present and future in one unitary gaze. They tend to be aware of their fantasy and dream life which form integral parts of their extended consciousness and are a source of new intuitions. This process of inner exploration has both a positive and a negative side. On the positive side they often pick up interesting and valuable information about the meaning and purpose of the inner man. But on the negative side, they can carry the process of inhibition of the endotonic and the mesotonic components to excess. The introverted intuition type has a tendency to withdraw too much from people. He becomes too wrapped up in his inner world and has no time for normal social contacts. He becomes reclusive and aloof, and people sensing these qualities feel rebuffed and rebuff him in return, but he sees only their rejection and not the reason for it. He then uses this rejection as a justification to socially isolate himself even more. This does not mean that the introverted intuition type would enjoy the same social gatherings as the extraverted sensation type, but in his own way he needs people around him. These contacts usually take the form of a few good friends where deep relationships develop.

The introverted intuition type has a tendency not to act, or put in another way, he is very active mentally but slow to act physically, especially when faced with a repetitive physical task. He tends to hold himself aloof from ordinary chores, partly because he is oblivious to them and partly because he feels he is engaged interiorly in something more important. It is as if he has to disengage his attention and specially focus it on the external job to be done before he can react and do it. But he cannot withdraw from the physical world and live exclusively within. He should make a special effort to become competent in those skills which most of the rest of the world take for granted, like cooking, building a bookcase, doing minor repairs on his car, etc. These are all ways of developing the mesotonic extraversion of action. Naturally the more mesomorphic introverted intuition types will tend to have less problems with doing things, but more problems with people, while with the more endomorphic introverted intuition types, the tendency will be reversed. The balanced introverted intuition types with a good endowment of each of the three temperamental components are often very capable in all areas, but suffer from an inability to decide what they really want to do.

The Psychological Type

The introverted intuition type who does not make

use of his second function of either thinking or feeling can wander in a world of interior images or ideas without trying to organize or evaluate them. A more systematic approach to the inner possibilities helps counterbalance the urge to be always running to see what is beyond the next interior hill. The introverted intuition type needs to make the attempt to discover the basic structure and interrelationships in the mass of inner images and ideas that usually present themselves to him. This makes the inner world more useful to him when he acts upon it and communicates it.

Whether he likes it or not, and he often doesn't, the introverted intuition type lives in this world and must learn how to relate to it. The introverted intuition type has already developed a way of relating to the world as he grew up by use of his conscious functions, which Jung called a persona, but his persona could never answer the question, "What is really my place in this world?", or "Can I really have a life in this world without it contradicting my inner world?" The answer to these questions is related to the integration of the other side of the personality. The bridge to the other side is often either extraverted feeling or extraverted thinking with overtones of sensation. The overtones spring from the connection the third function has with the extraverted sensation of the fourth. The other side when unintegrated manifests itself in a fear of being engulfed and enslaved by the world.

The extraverted nature of the third function often presents itself in the form of having an actual relationship with someone of the opposite sex, and the challenge of the fourth function can be found in dealing directly with simple sensation realities. For the more extraverted type, these ordinary everyday things seem hardly worth noting, but for the introverted intuition type, because the fourth function is filled with the unconscious, they can have a mysteri-

ous and frightening quality which makes it very difficult to deal with them in a straight-forward objective
manner.

The Extraverted Intuition Type

The Body Type

The extraverted intuition types are highly active
people, for they not only have something new they
must be doing but they have the mesomorphy to
sustain their extraverted action. Often they will not
take time to eat properly and they have their meals
on the run. The lack of a proper diet probably
accentuates their changeability; they lack the endomorph's weight which might have slowed them down
a bit. They also lack the endomorph's bodily relaxation. Their muscles are in a state of tension as if
they must be ready to charge off at a moment's
notice. A set time for meals together, with a carefully chosen balanced diet, with the meals eaten
without a sense of rush, are all good goals for the
more extreme extraverted intuition type.

Extraverted intuition types share the introverted
intuition type's fascination for new possibilities, but
not his inclination for quiet time. Quiet time for
themselves is about last on their list of priorities,
but this is the doorway to the world within. They
have to learn to stop so the body and psyche can
catch up.

The Temperament Type

The extraverted intuition types can be pleasant
company, for they can be bubbling over with new
adventures and they have a knack of projecting their
feelings into a social situation and warming it much
like the extraverted feeling type. This is not the
more diffused amiability of the extraverted sensation

type; it is more highly focused and in the service of the primary intuition. They tend to turn their feelings on and off according to whether the situation has intuitive possibilities for them or not. They have to learn that their friends want a constancy of feeling tone and attention even when they themselves are in a rush to be off on new adventures.

Their ectotonia is bound up with their intuition rather than their self-reflection. This they tend to avoid like their brother extraverts, and their highly-tuned antennae are outwardly directed rather than inwardly, as with the introverted intuition types. Their constant future orientation does not give them time to reflect on what is happening to their lives here and now under the impact of the headlong rush. They need time for their ectotonia to assert itself so they can see what price the people around them are paying, as well as the burden their own body is carrying.

The Psychological Type

The extraverted intuition type, even with the aid of the helping functions, cannot really deal with his other side effectively, for all these functions have an extraverted character to the degree they are integrated with the conscious personality. This same sort of cleavage exists in all the types, and the initial reorientation of attitude is one of the most decisive battles that must be fought. The conscious attitude has become solidified over the years so that the habitual way of dealing with problems is in terms of more of the same. What is necessary is a new attitude, but this feels like an affront and insult to consciousness, and so it is resisted. For the extraverted intuition type the other side is characterized by introverted thinking or feeling and introverted sensation. Instead of letting introverted sensation batter him from the outside, the extraverted intuition thinking type has to try to approach it through the mediation of the lower third function which asks, "How do I personally feel about all these intuitions?" "How can I evaluate them for myself?" And deeper down he has to submit to letting himself look at his sense impressions in order to establish a relationship to his inner world through them.

The Introverted Sensation Type

The Body Type

The introverted sensation type with his ecto-morph-endomorph physique is inclined to put on extra weight, but not apparently to the extent of the extraverted sensation type. The extra weight, how-ever, is enough to increase the inhibition of his mesomorphic component which is already being held in check by the introverted sensation itself. The introverted sensation type is often a slow reactor, and he does not need any extra obstacles.

The introverted sensation type shares the ecto-morph's love of quiet, but most of the quiet is taken up with sense impressions which do not incline them to movement in the way the intuitions of the intro-verted intuition type often spill over into going somewhere new. The introverted sensation type has to be careful not to build a cocoon from which he has difficulty emerging.

The Temperament Type

The introverted sensation types show little of the open love of people of the extraverted sensation type. They have good feeling tone, but often find it difficult to express these feelings freely and be demonstrative with them. They have to work at being more dramatic than their personal inclination, based on a realization that the world around them measures feeling by the extraverted feeling of the extraverted feeling type and the extraverted sensation type, and so has difficulty believing that they really do have feelings at all.

They work in a highly meticulous and organized way. Their own experience of working with other people should be enough to show them that their work style differs from others. This should be accepted as a simple fact without judging if the other person is doing a good job by the exacting introverted sensation type standards. There are other standards that have to do with speed, sociability while working, etc., which if they cannot emulate because of their own gift, they can learn to appreciate and thus lessen the tension of working with other types.

The Psychological Type

The introverted sensation type with the help of the second and third functions makes his way in the world as a good and steady worker. This is the persona that he presents, his extraverted mask, while beneath it he lives in his introverted world. But neither the persona nor the conscious introverted personality is fully adequate for all the situations. The introverted sensation type can be stuck in his current situation because of inertia and a lack of development of the other side which would give him access to more extraverted energies, particularly extraverted intuition.

Often the development of the other side of the introverts, since it has an extraverted character, is associated with outer events. For the introverted sensation type and the introverted intuition type courtship and marriage can represent a difficult challenge precisely because it is not a matter-of-fact reality, but intimately linked with their third function of extraverted feeling or thinking which is often quite undeveloped. The development of the other side of the introvert is not simply the adjustment to the demands of the outer world but a simultaneous development of a deeper part of his personality which he needs in order to make the outer adjustment.

Extraverted feeling or thinking is the bridge to dealing with extraverted intuition for the introverted sensation type. And extraverted intuition is the way the introverted sensation type not only deals with questions of "What new job should I take?" or "What new life-style should I adopt?", but it is also at the same time the medium by which the introverted sensation type deals with the legitimate demands of the inner world and begins to balance the one-sidedness of consciousness with a relationship to both the outer and inner world.

The Extraverted Feeling Type

The Body Type

The extraverted feeling type has many similarities with the extraverted thinking type, as we have already noted. She does not have to be told to exercise, but weight gain for those along the extraverted sensation line is equally dangerous to their health. She shares the extraverted thinking type's lack of quiet time, and as more and more extraverted feeling types enter the male competitive arenas they will tend to show the extraverted thinking type's difficulty in relaxing, sleeping, taking time to eat, etc. Hopefully their higher degree of endomorphy will help keep them from the worst excesses.

The Temperament Type

The extraverted feeling type with too little to do, either because she is held back by stereotypes about women's roles in the world or by her own inability to think up what to do, has no real outlet for her mesotonia. Her ability for energetic action can be frittered away on inconsequential activities and leave her unsatisfied. The extraverted feeling type who takes her place in the world alongside the extraverted thinking type avoids this problem but has to face the problems of the working mesotonic. The mesotonic in a career position can develop tunnel vision and compulsive drive that begins to ignore the enjoyment of people because they are people and family as family, and subordinate everything to the job to be done.

The emphasis on mesotonia in the extraverted feeling type gives rise to the paradox of the unfeeling feeler, which is the counterpart of the ruthlessness and callousness sometimes found in the extraverted thinking type. The extraverted feeling becomes more and more one-sided and since it is cut off from the rest of the personality, it lacks new creative energies and becomes narrower and narrower in application. It loses a certain flexibility of being nice in general and becomes nice for definite motives, and thus appears calculating and cold when seen from outside the focus of feeling attention.

The Psychological Type

The other side of the extraverted feeling type is introverted thinking, which is approached by either introverted sensation or introverted intuition. Both of these approaches take time and reflection in order to perceive what the contents of the inner world are, and that these contents are as worthy of attention as the outer world. The extraverted feeling type is quick to find substitutes for her own thought. She tends to take up as her own what society thinks. If this process is not broken by inner development, then a change of social setting does not necessarily lead to meaningful change, but simply to the adoption of another ready-made body of thought. The extraverted feeling type has to reach the point of saying, "What do I really think?" "What is my personal philosophy of life?" This is very different from taking up some philosophy ready-made and saying, "This is my philosophy now." A personal standpoint has to be worked out step-by-step by a dialogue between the conscious and the unconscious. The result might be of modest size, but it will be real and effective for the person who has created it.

The Introverted Thinking and the Introverted Feeling Types

The Body Types

We have seen the wide divergence of body types that distinguishes the introverted thinking intuition type from the introverted thinking sensation type and the introverted feeling intuition type from the introverted feeling sensation type. The introverted thinking intuition type shares many of the problems of the introverted intuition thinking type, especially if his ectomorphy is pronounced. He has more mesomorphy and thus can sustain exercise better, but he should tend to a modified version of the introverted intuition thinking type's sleep and diet habits. This holds as well for the introverted feeling intuition type of high ectomorphy. Extra weight and relaxation will help them express their low endomorphic component better, and protect them from overstimulation.

The introverted thinking sensation type and the introverted feeling sensation type have a tendency to put on weight and become heavy-set or beefy, and can follow a modified version of the extraverted sensation type diet. Both the introverted thinking sensation/introverted feeling sensation type and the introverted thinking intuition/introverted feeling intuition type value quiet and privacy.

The Temperament Type

The introverted thinking types show little of the indiscriminate amiability of the endotonic. This is more noticeable in the introverted thinking sensation type than it is in the introverted thinking intuition type, for we instinctively expect the more endomorphic personality to express more amiability. Introverted thinking sensation types have a strong mesotonic component, but it is expressed not in the action of the extraverted thinking type but in a mental way. They are decisive thinkers and careful planners and make formidable competitors. They have to strive to allow their endotonia to come out, and simply enjoy the people around them, especially in the forms that are most distant to inner intellectuality like children, pets, etc.

The introverted feeling sensation type and the introverted feeling intuition type are blessed with abundant feelings, but since they flow inwardly, they have to make an extra effort to let their endotonia come out and let the people around them know that they have feelings by vocalizing and demonstrating them.

The Psychological Type

The introverted thinking type with thinking aided by the second and third functions can be effective and efficient both within his world of ideas and in their application. His persona of the thinking man is appreciated in our society. The introverted feeling types, however, seem to have more difficulty because they are judged more critically according to the extraverted feeling type norms of society. Their persona often appears less adequately developed from this point of view.

But the introverted thinking types and the introverted feeling types, in common with the rest of the introverts, need to make a more adequate contact with the outer world than what their one-sided persona allows. This contact and adaptation to the outer world is simultaneously one of relation to the inner world as well. There are situations which will demand an extraverted third function of sensation or intuition, as well as contact with an extraverted fourth function of feeling or thinking as the case may be.

The introverted thinking types must develop the ability to consciously contact their extraverted feeling side and use it to maintain the feeling tone with the people around them, especially those outside of their inner circle. The introverted feeling types must develop the extraverted thinking dimension of their personality, which, on the outside, represents the ability to plan and act effectively and logically and see how the world works, and thus avoid succumbing to a magical kind of thought which grips them and takes the place of real thinking. But the fourth function in each is not simply a way of better outer adaptation; it is the path of inner adaptation as well, and through it the introverted thinking types answer the questions, "How do I feel about myself?" "What are my values for my own life?" And the introverted feeling types develop their personal philosophies, much like we have seen in the case of the extraverted feeling type.

BIBLIOGRAPHY

Adler, Gerhard. (1961). **The Living Symbol.** A Case Study in the Process of Individuation. New York: Pantheon Books, Inc.

Arraj, Tyra and James. (1987). **A Jungian Psychology Resource Guide.** Chiloquin, OR: Tools for Inner Growth.

_____(1987). **The Treasures of Simple Living.** Chiloquin, OR: Tools for Inner Growth.

Brown, Tom. (1978). **The Tracker.** New York: Prentice-Hall.

_____(1980). **The Search.** New York: Prentice-Hall.

Franz, Marie-Louise von. (1971). "The Inferior Function" in **Jung's Typology.** New York: Spring Publications.

Jung, C.G. (1913). "A Contribution to the Study of Psychological Types." **Coll. Works,** 6. Princeton, NJ: Princeton University Press.

_____(1921). "Psychological Types." **Coll. Works,** 6. Princeton, NJ: Princeton University Press.

_____(1923). "Psychological Types." **Coll. Works,** 6. Princeton, NJ: Princeton University Press.

_____(1928). **The Relations Between the Ego and the Unconscious.** Coll. Works, 7. Princeton, NJ: Princeton University Press.

_____(1931). "A Psychological Theory of Types." **Coll. Works,** 6. Princeton, NJ: Princeton University Press.

_____(1934/1950). "A Study in the Process of Individuation." **Coll. Works,** 9, Part I. Princeton, NJ: Princeton University Press.

_____(1936). "Psychological Typology." **Coll. Works,** 6. Princeton, NJ: Princeton University

Press.

_____(1950). "Concerning Mandala Symbolism."
Coll. Works, 9, Part I. Princeton, NJ: Princeton
University Press.

_____(1961). **Memories, Dreams, Reflections.** New
York: Vintage Books.

_____(1968). **Man and His Symbols.** New York:
Dell.

Neumann, Erich. (1969). **Depth Psychology and a New
Ethic.** New York: Harper & Row.

Schwarzenegger, Arnold. (1977). **Arnold: The Education
of a Bodybuilder.** New York: Simon and Schuster

Sheldon, W.H. (with the collaboration of Stevens, S.S.
and Tucker, W.B.) (1940). **The Varieties of Human
Physique:** An Introduction to Constitutional
Psychology. New York: Harper.

_____(with the collaboration of Stevens, S.S.)
(1942). **The Varieties of Temperament:** A Psychology of Constitutional Differences. New York:
Harper.

_____(with the collaboration of Dupertuis, C.W.
and McDermott, E.) (1954). **Atlas of Men:** A Guide
for Somatotyping the Adult Male at All Ages.
New York: Harper.

Note: See **Volume II** of **Tracking the Elusive Human**
for an extensive bibliography.

INDEX

A JUNGIAN PSYCHOLOGY
RESOURCE GUIDE

Compiled by Tyra Arraj and James Arraj

This unique reference work to Jungian Psychology today describes:

Local and Professional Groups in the United
      States and Canada
Local and Professional Groups Around the World
Psychological Types Organizations
Conferences
Periodicals
Book Publishers
Mail Order Book Sources
Libraries and Bibliographical Tools
Basic Reading List and Films
Jungian Analysis and Training Programs

It shows you where to find the answers to:
Who was C.G. Jung? What did he say? How can I get a real picture of what he was like? How can I get an idea of books and articles that exist about Jung's psychology? Where can I get books on Jungian psychology? Where do I look when starting research on a topic in Jungian psychology? Where can I find a Jungian analyst? Where can I meet people interested in Jung? What periodicals exist in Jungian psychology or with Jungian-oriented material? What is Jungian Analysis like? How can I find the up-to- date programs of U.S. local and professional groups? How can I keep track of the activities of foreign professional groups?

144 pages, paperback, index, $11.95
ISBN 0-914073-05-2

ST. JOHN OF THE CROSS AND DR. C. G. JUNG

CHRISTIAN MYSTICISM
IN THE LIGHT OF
JUNGIAN PSYCHOLOGY

BY JAMES ARRAJ

Many current attempts to revitalize the life of prayer are inspired by either the writings of St. John of the Cross or the psychology of Dr. C. G. Jung. Both are excellent choices. Even better would be a program of renewal under their joint inspiration.

Yet such a program faces three serious challenges: theological misgivings about the compatibility of Jung's psychology with Christian belief, long-standing misinterpretations of St. John's doctrine on contemplation, and the need to clarify the relationship between Jung's process of individuation and contemplation.

Parts I and II are devoted to resolving these first two problems, while Part III gives a practical demonstration of the relationship between individuation and contemplation in St. John's life and writings and in a variety of contemporary spiritual problems.

Let me put it more concretely. I am enthusiastic about the prospect of using Jung and St. John as practical guides in the interior life. But when this enthusiasm begins to run away with me I see Victor White deep in conversation with Jung in the tower at Bollingen and their subsequent estrangement. Or I see Juan Falconi and Antonio Rojas in the Madrid of the late 1620's evoking the name of John of the Cross with the best of intentions to fuel a popular enthusiasm for contemplation, yet paving the road that led to a distrust of mysticism that has lingered to our own day.

Although these problems are serious and will force us to take a difficult journey through the thickets of epistemology and the history of spiritual life in the 17th century, I believe they are surmountable and will help lay foundations for a renewal of the life of prayer and a practical science of spiritual direction.

FROM THE INTRODUCTION

200 pages, 5 1/2 x 8 1/2, paperback original, index, bibliography, notes, ISBN 0-914073-02-8, $11.95.

THE TREASURES OF SIMPLE LIVING

A FAMILY'S SEARCH FOR A SIMPLER AND MORE MEANINGFUL LIFE IN THE MIDDLE OF A FOREST

by TYRA ARRAJ with JAMES ARRAJ

Our future was set out for us: full-time jobs, mortgage payments for the next 20 years, and retirement at 65. Our children would go to school and we would see them as much as our busy schedules allowed. But such a future held no attraction for us. So we packed up, left it all behind and drove into the unknown.

Our journey took us beyond the electric lines, telephone, paved roads and television. We built our own house, grew salads year-round in a solar greenhouse and taught our children at home, all in the midst of a forest where the nearest neighbors are wild animals and the snow gets four feet deep.

The inconveniences were soon forgotten in the joys of living under our own roof, watching our children blossom and discovering abilities we never knew we had. The simplicity took away economic pressures and gave us time to search for life's deeper meanings.

PART I explains why we left the city, how we solved the problem of earning a living and what we went through once we bought a piece of land in the middle of a forest. Read about: the rat race, searching for land, house-building, alternative utilities, a greenhouse-bioshelter, tofu and tempeh, life without a television and home school.

PART II tells about the treasures we found in our simple life, why our experiment paid us back a thousand-fold, and the dream of a bioshelter community.

PART III describes common obstacles to creating a new lifestyle closer to nature, and some important skills like crafts, economic basics, orthomolecular medicine, and human differences, that helped us along the way.

PART IV is a **Resource Guide** for those who might like to begin their own adventure in simple living, including books and organizations on the subjects covered in the first three sections.

FROM THE INTRODUCTION

216 pages, 5 1/2 x 8 1/2, paperback original, resource guide, 14 line drawings, index
ISBN 0-914073-04-4, $11.95.

COMING SOON:

TRACKING THE ELUSIVE HUMAN

VOLUME II

by JAMES ARRAJ

ORDER FORM

Please send me:

Quantity	Title	Price
_____	Tracking the Elusive Human, Vol. 1	$11.95
_____	St. John of the Cross & Dr. C.G. Jung	$11.95
_____	A Jungian Psychology Resource Guide	$11.95
_____	The Treasures of Simple Living	$11.95

Add $1.00 for the first book and $.50 for each additional book. Enclosed is my check/money order for $_____

NAME_____

STREET_____

CITY_____STATE_____ZIP_____

Send to: INNER GROWTH BOOKS
Box 520
Chiloquin, OR 97624

ORDER FORM

Please send me:

Quantity	Title	Price
_____	Tracking the Elusive Human, Vol. 1	$11.95
_____	St. John of the Cross & Dr. C.G. Jung	$11.95
_____	A Jungian Psychology Resource Guide	$11.95
_____	The Treasures of Simple Living	$11.95

Add $1.00 for the first book and $.50 for each additional book. Enclosed is my check/money order for $_____

NAME_____

STREET_____

CITY_____STATE_____ZIP_____

Send to: INNER GROWTH BOOKS
Box 520
Chiloquin, OR 97624

ORDER FORM

Please send me:

Quantity	Title	Price
_____	Tracking the Elusive Human, Vol. 1	$11.95
_____	St. John of the Cross & Dr. C.G. Jung	$11.95
_____	A Jungian Psychology Resource Guide	$11.95
_____	The Treasures of Simple Living	$11.95

Add $1.00 for the first book and $.50 for each additional book. Enclosed is my check/money order for
$_____

NAME_____

STREET_____

CITY_____STATE_____ZIP_____

Send to: INNER GROWTH BOOKS
Box 520
Chiloquin, OR 97624

ORDER FORM

Please send me:

Quantity	Title	Price
_____	Tracking the Elusive Human, Vol. 1	$11.95
_____	St. John of the Cross & Dr. C.G. Jung	$11.95
_____	A Jungian Psychology Resource Guide	$11.95
_____	The Treasures of Simple Living	$11.95

Add $1.00 for the first book and $.50 for each additional book. Enclosed is my check/money order for
$_____

NAME_____

STREET_____

CITY_____STATE_____ZIP_____

Send to: INNER GROWTH BOOKS
Box 520
Chiloquin, OR 97624

ABOUT THE AUTHORS

Jim and Tyra Arraj live with their children deep in a forest far from paved roads and power lines near Crater Lake, Oregon. There they built their own house, grow vegetables in a solar greenhouse, survive 4 feet of snow in the winter and write books about simple living, Jungian psychology, philosophy and religion.